Tennis, Anyone?
The Wimps's Guide to Tennis and Other Racquet Sports

James B. Kobak, Jr.

Copyright © 2024 by James B. Kobak, Jr.
All rights reserved. No part of this book may be used or reproduced in any manner whatsoever without written permission, except in the case of brief quotations embodied in critical articles or reviews.

Cover: Design by Dwayne Booth
Book layout by HumorOutcasts Press

Published 2024 by HumorOutcasts Press
Printed in the United States of America

ISBN: 979-8-9894863-5-9

Acknowledgements

Thanks to HumorOutcasts Press and everyone on the publishing team, especially Donna Cavanagh for her patience, encouragement and expertise; Kathryn Taylor for her editorial corrections, suggestions and advice; Dwayne Booth for the ideas and execution of the cover design.

And special thanks to my wife, Carol, for putting up with me for years not only on the tennis court but as I scribbled and asked for comments on the various pieces that eventually became the manuscript for this little book which I hope readers will enjoy.

Table of Contents

Tennis, Anyone?.. 1
The History of Tennis 5
The Rules of Tennis.. 14
What the Beginner Needs to Know About the Official Code of Tennis
.... 20
A Preliminary Tennis Quiz 23
The Art of Picking Up the Ball 27
Choosing a Tennis Racquet... 30
Strokes... 34
Other Tennis Gear 45
Tennis Drills 51
Getting in Shape to Play Tennis 57
A Tennis Villanelle.. 63
Meet the Backboard: Your Tennis Bestie 65
Tennis Strategy... 71
Variety: The Spice of Life and Racquet Sports............................ 75
The Racquet Sport Intelligence Test... 85
A Short Poetry Break.. 89
Tennis and Culture: The Sociology of Tennis 91
Professional Tennis and You... 95
A Poetic Coda to Professional Tennis and You: The Torments of the
Tournaments..100
Using Artificial Intelligence to Improve Your Tennis.................102
Tennis Meets STEM: What Developments Like the Space Telescope
Mean for Racquet Sports...107
The Culinary Aspects of Tennis and Other Racquet Sports 110

The Rules Quiz	116
Another Tennis Villanelle	119
Tennis and Theology	121
Looking Ahead: Some Thoughts About the Future of Racquet Sports	126
An Ode to My Tennis Partners	131
GLOSSARY	133

James B. Kobak, Jr.

Tennis, Anyone?

Tennis, anyone? These words are said to have first been uttered by Humphrey Bogart in the movie *Sabrina*. They sound innocent enough but, like Bogart in the movie *The Maltese Falcon*, they carry with them menace and a hint of danger.

People who do not buy this book will unhesitatingly answer *yes* to the question "Tennis, anyone?" and run off to buy a racquet and other tennis paraphernalia. Only years later will these unfortunate souls be seen again, dazed, bedraggled, bathed in perspiration, badly sunburned, and clutching their latest tennis racquets to their chests because of the heart attack suffered upon learning the cost of the racquets. These wretched creatures are likely to face a lifetime of penury, pulled muscles, unpleasant companions, and penitential weekends away from family and friends with only Power Bars and Gatorade to sustain them.

It is to be hoped that by perusing this book, you will at least hesitate before responding too cavalierly to any question with the word *tennis* in it. You will learn enough to pause; consider your options; and remember how pleasant it is to doze off on a Saturday afternoon while reading a book like this in a comfortable easy chair in an air-conditioned room in the presence of TV, food, and cases of previous years' Beaujolais nouveau. You will have time to remember how much easier, less embarrassing and more satisfying it is to watch and criticize others hitting backhands and overheads than it is to attempt to do these things yourself. You can take a few moments to reflect on the meaning

Tennis, Anyone?

of life, the purpose of your education, and how foolish, overweight, knock-kneed—in short, how much like Sidney Greenstreet in *The Maltese Falcon*—you look in shorts or a mini-tennis dress.

"Tennis, anyone?" is a question that only you can definitively answer for yourself. It is, however, well to bear in mind other phrases that begin with the word "tennis." These include "tennis elbow," "tennis injury," and "tennis bum." These words are not even questions, like "Tennis anyone?" They are unequivocal, affirmative statements derived from decades of human experience. They are ignored at your peril.

Tennis is a popular activity that can always be played at some small risk to life and limb—and much greater risk to pride and self-confidence. On the other band, because it is a popular activity, tennis can always be more safely read about in magazines, studied in books, and scrutinized on high definition TV. Thus, one approach to the game is signing up for more cable TV, plastering your walls with pictures of attractive tennis players from *Sports Illustrated* bathing suit issues, and buying and handing out to everyone you know who mentions the word "tennis" copies of *The Wimp's Guide to Tennis*. This is indeed the approach to the sport taken by the author. This approach saves time, energy, and anxiety and ensures that instead of throwing your money away on tennis pros and tennis gear, you throw it away on a far worthier, or at least needier, cause—me.

Of course it is possible that you have already thrown your

money away on tennis pros and tennis gear because you foolishly failed to make this book your first tennis-related purchase. Indeed, you may have failed to buy this book at all and are instead in the remainder section of some seedy second hand bookstore leafing through it to get to the exciting parts. You have gotten exactly what you deserve—in all probability including a rash of some kind from the last person to have leafed through the book—for flouting the cardinal rule of tennis or, for that matter any, activity involving physical exercise and dexterity: it is always preferable to spend a lifetime studying it than a morning or afternoon doing it. Do you suppose it is mere coincidence that for two weeks every summer tens of thousands of people go to the Wimbledon grounds but only a handful ever set foot on the courts—and that handful is paid to do so?

If you have been imprudent enough to purchase tennis equipment, all is not irretrievably lost. Much of this equipment can be recycled for other uses. Tennis balls, for example, are excellent for playing fetch with golden retrievers, although this will require acquiring a golden retriever. (Playing fetch without a golden retriever quickly becomes tiring, and it is unlikely that you will slobber all over the ball as thoroughly as a golden retriever does.) The tennis shoes you have bought can then be thrown at the golden retriever when you tire of playing fetch before the retriever does, or when the retriever is the neighbor's dog and turns out to be a Rottweiler. The retriever will also enjoy gnawing on the shoes when you fall asleep after an exciting afternoon of fetch. Just remember to take the shoes off before falling asleep.

One way to handle the question "Tennis, anyone?" is mentally to substitute other famous phrases and act accordingly. Especially recommended for this purpose are these warnings: "Beware the Ides of March," about not playing with anyone in a tennis dress that resembles a toga; T.S. Eliot's well known line from *The Wasteland*, "I will show you fear in a handful of dust" about the fun of playing on clay courts; and the universal threat "Your ass is grass" about playing on slippery grass courts with people who turn out to be former camp counselors and Marine drill sergeants.

Good responses to the question "Tennis, anyone?" should include "Nyet," "No way, José," and "Sez who?," depending on whether the question is asked in the Russian Tea Room, a Mexican restaurant, or the cafeteria at a Canarsie high school. If asked this question while running for President of the United States, say, "Read my lips" and instruct your lawyer to file briefs in the United States Supreme Court so that the votes of Florida tennis players will not be counted. Then, as President, you can declare your tennis opponents terrorists, lock them up at Guantanamo Bay and throw away the key, use the White House tennis court exclusively for Easter egg hunts, and become what so many aspiring tennis players eventually become: a golfer.

Jim Kobak

The History of Tennis

The sport we now know as tennis can be traced to two distinct origins: a European source in the courts and monasteries of the French nobility and an American source in the savage ball game of the ancient Aztecs. Because of these origins, tennis has always mixed conservative, elitist European traditions with more populist, democratic New World tendencies.

The European game had rules as complicated as chess and was played on a bizarre court designed by the Marquis de Sade for chasing women dressed as French maids. The European game was originally called *jeu de paume*, from the phrase "I will crush you with the palm of my hand," which the Marquis de Sade used to say to the French maids and Louis the XIV used to say to his courtiers at the start of a game. This game is called real or court tennis today by the eleven people in the world who still play it. Chasing the French maids is now called reality TV.

The French tried playing a simplified version of *jeu de paume* on a barge, but it sank at Le Havre. Thereafter only Jean Jacques Cousteau much enjoyed playing underwater, and even he had no way of calling an opponent's shot out without drowning. Tennis was important enough in Europe that the Dauphin of France sent Henry the Fifth of Great Britain a can of tennis balls to compensate for taking much of his land and property. When the soggy balls failed to bounce, the incensed Henry slew thousands of Frenchmen at Agincourt, making

Tennis, Anyone?

a famous speech comparing the balls of English men to those of Frenchmen, a comparison many Englishmen repeat to this day.

In the Aztec ball game, by contrast, hundreds of matches were played simultaneously on the same court. This was because no one could decipher the Aztec system of writing, and players therefore had no way to determine who had actually signed up for the court. Losers in these ancient Aztec matches were not only crushed in the palm of a king's hand but had their hearts cut out and eaten, making it quite a chore to sweep the court after a match and even more difficult to maintain a regular Tuesday tennis group. Notwithstanding these drawbacks, the Aztecs introduced several improvements to the French game, including the invention of rubber, which allowed the balls actually to bounce; the use of a lightweight machete as a forerunner to the tennis racquet; and the sale of nachos and quesadillas in the refreshment stand.

As every school child knows, the aristocratic Old World and populist New World strains of tennis were finally reconciled in the famous Tennis Court Oath administered at Versailles in the eighteenth century. As a result, the French revolution occurred. French maids in the United States became waitresses at Hooters, and the game of court tennis was confined to an ancient regime, which consisted of sommeliers at over-priced restaurants and Charles de Gaulle. The bourgeoisie laid claim to Robespierre, Marat, *Les Miz*, the province of Quebec, and an outdoor tennis game. Later, in the Russian Revolution,

Jim Kobak

Lenin declared that the masses should have an indoor game as well, leading to squash and racquetball. Hippies in the 1960s applied these revolutionary principles while on acid and ended up with badminton and a ball that isn't round and has feathers. As the hippies aged and feathers fell off the badminton ball (called a shuttlecock), the world was introduced to pickle ball, a game supposedly named after a dog named "Pickles" who liked chasing after the defeathered whiffle balls used in the game. This has left tennis historians with a so far unanswerable question: why would anyone name a dog "Pickles?"

Since Versailles, tennis has become a more exhilarating, more accessible, more widely known sport. Oaths of various kinds uttered on the court, however, have remained one of its most ubiquitous features.

The new people's tennis had a few growing pains. A Major Winfield laid out official dimensions for tennis courts in 1875 but, being the repressed Victorian that he was, had other things, such as Mrs. Winfield, on his subconscious. He gave his tennis court an hourglass shape and called it a Sphairistike. That may explain why Major Winfield was not General or even Lieutenant Colonel Winfield. Tennis assumed its present rectangular configuration and name a few years later, thanks to a civilian Wimbledon groundskeeper with a flat-chested, no nonsense spouse.

At this point tennis spread through Europe and America like crabgrass in Scarsdale, causing it to be referred to as lawn tennis. Now great performers, like the Sears brothers, Big Bill Tilden, and the

Tennis, Anyone?

French "three Musketeers," appeared in exciting competitions like Wimbledon, the Davis Cup, and Newport. Suzanne Langhorne Langley took off her petticoats and went flying through the air like an Isadora Duncan dancer according to all the old photographs. Bunny Austin, Fred Perry's doubles partner, replaced his flannel trousers with shorts. Henri LaCoste played in short-sleeved alligator shirts. Gussy Moran showed up at Wimbledon in gold lamé tennis panties. Players were playing harder and taking off clothes right and left. And that was before Anna Kournikova, Janet Jackson, or internet porn sites.

Pictures of some of these early players show them holding slender racquets that seem unusual today because they were made of a substance known as wood. This substance was found in places known as forests containing objects known as trees. Fortunately, these were removed years ago in favor of oil derricks, allowing tennis racquets to be made out of more pliant, more synthetic and more expensive materials.

Patience Outerbridge introduced the game to the United States, where it was played on a bridge, the Outerbridge Crossing. Unfortunately, the bridge was not only windy, but also open to automobile traffic, wreaking havoc on players' timing and reducing their numbers through accidents. Moreover, players at one end of the court had to pay a toll every time they came to the net, while those at the other were sometimes arrested for jaywalking.

As the game spread, suitable lawns were chewed up or used for golf courses, so substitute surfaces had to be found. A French brick maker whose design for a brick Eiffel Tower had been passed over found a use for his surplus bricks and vented much of his Gallic frustration by taking the bricks to the top of the Eiffel Tower as soon as it opened and dropping them on the design committee. The bricks pulverized into slow French red clay on which the design committee's heirs have had to play endless points while ruining their tennis sneakers. Many hard and composite surfaces have subsequently been invented by orthopedic surgeons to guarantee a continuous demand for knee surgery.

Tennis was originally an amateur sport, but over time it became enmeshed in under-the-table payments and disguised appearance fees collectively denigrated as "shamateurism." To remove the taint of shamateurism, tennis competitions were opened to declared professionals. The under-the-table transfers and disguised fees migrated to politics and became known as campaign financing.

A number of star players and strong personalities have fueled the growth of tennis in the twentieth century. These include Margaret Smith Court, Arthur Ashe, Pancho Gonzalez, and "Little Mo" Connolly, the often forgotten fourth Stooge. In the 1960s, Renee Richards, an ophthalmologist with an uncanny taste for ugly eyeglasses, had a sex change operation to be able to play on the women's tour, showing the lengths to which players would go to avoid

Tennis, Anyone?

playing against the tempestuous Ilie Nastase. Players emerged from diverse countries and backgrounds. These included the graceful native Australian, Yvonne Goolagong; the dreadlocked African, Yannick Noah; the Queen of Wimbledon, Maria Bueno, a Brazilian; the Peruvian, Alex Olmedo; the flying Dutchman, Tom Okker, who emerged from Wagnerian opera; and Vitas Gerulaitis who emerged from who knows where the morning of a match.

A famous match occurred in the Houston Astrodome in 1969 when Billy Jean King, a woman player with a pioneering spirit, beat Bobby Riggs, a man actually old enough to have been a pioneer. Truth to tell, it wasn't much of a match, with King winning easily, but it sparked interest in tennis clothing, women's issues, and how much money tennis players make, all staples of the game today. Epic struggles also ensued between the brooding Swedish baseliner, Bjorn Borg, and the dyspeptic American server and volleyer, John McEnroe. These matches had a Shakespearean quality, with Hamlet on one side of the net and Mercutio with a New York accent on the other. A similar phenomenon developed in the women's game whenever Chris Evert played Martina Navratilova. The matches between these two great women players took place during the Cold War and were closely monitored by military authorities after Navratilova defected to the West. Even though Navratilova was using her free time to take skiing lessons at Aspen, the Russian tennis federation was convinced she was practicing with Lyndon Johnson and Richard Nixon on the White

Jim Kobak

House tennis court. When Navratilova rushed the net at set point during an Easter Bowl Tournament in Miami, Evert hit a high defensive lob into a southeasterly breeze and triggered the Cuban missile crisis. The crisis was resolved only through secret diplomatic channels—namely, Charlie Pasarell, who explained to Fidel Castro that the situation was comparable to Dean Rusk hitting a foul ball after being badly fooled and swinging like a rusty gate at one of Castro's curve balls.

Ultimately the genes and prize money of all the great tennis players were pooled and given to the Williams sisters, allowing them to play each other at peak television time and eliminating the distraction of other players with hard to pronounce names. To save money, the sisters even design and sew their own clothes the night before each match. The distractions are now provided by numerous announcers who comment on the sisters' every move and facial expression.

Meanwhile tennis on the men's side came to be dominated by the famous triumvirate of Roger Federer, Rafael Nadal, and Novak Djokovic. "Veni, vidi, vici," said Federer after coming down from Transalpine Gaul to defeat Vercingetorix in a series of the grand slams in the years MMMVI to MMXIX AD, thereby seizing control of the other parts of Gaul now called the European Union, as well as the island of Corsica and the Rolex watch company. As Virgil praised the emperor Augustus, so did pundits descended from Edward Gibbons apotheosize the great Swiss tennis player Federer as a godlike philosopher king. But before being declared a god, Federer crossed the

Tennis, Anyone?

Rubicon once too often and lost some matches to the young Spanish pretender, Rafael Nadal.

Still as a young man, Nadal went on to conquer tennis stadiums in several continents, along with their attendant duchies, satrapies, and allies. His great naval Armada sailed toward the British Isles, threatening the Crown, the Exchequer and even Wimbledon itself. The well-known sportswriter Shakespeare described him as having a lean and hungry look, and eventually the rigors of play took their toil, exiling the fierce Spaniard to a Mediterranean island where he is rumored even now to be plotting a desperate escape and comeback.

So for now it is the third of the triumvirs, Novak Djokovic, who bestrides the world as its remaining tennis colossus. "Ave atque vale," says each new gladiator forced to succumb to his will and his guile. But, as Gibbons reminds us, no empire and no emperor endures forever, and even now some new, rude beast—whether it be an Alcaraz, a Rublev, or some obscure pickle ball player from the Hamptons—slouches toward Queens or Australia to be born. Who it will be and when it will come, not even Edward Gibbon or Shakespeare could tell, only the fullness of time and future editions of this book.

Tennis has come a long way since the Dark Ages of the sport when court tennis balls had to be made fastidiously by hand and still did not bounce. Now the world machine produces more than twenty five million cans of rubberized tennis balls annually, more than even you could hit over a fence or into a net in a lifetime. If these balls were laid end to end they would circle the globe at the equator and become a menace to international shipping.

Tennis now spans the globe with evermore imaginative, evermore costly racquets and clothing. It is only a matter of time before tennis will be played in outer space. Then tennis will indeed have achieved its full potential: court time will become even more expensive, lack of gravity will make it even harder to keep the ball in the court, and one will find oneself playing with not one, but several suns in one's eyes.

Tennis, Anyone?

The Rules of Tennis

One thing that makes tennis frustrating and confusing for many players is the plethora of rules that govern the game. Unlike cricket, one cannot hit the ball almost anywhere and have it count; unlike lacrosse, one cannot carry the ball around on the strings of the racquet indefinitely and run into other players willy-nilly; and unlike field hockey, one cannot simply roll the ball along the grass while whacking young women on the shins with a heavy stick. Tennis is a highly structured endeavor with precise rules and regulations, much like a divorce proceeding or military court martial, except that there is no habeas corpus, no right to counsel, and no alimony to receive at the end.

A tennis game begins when one player serves from the right side of the baseline. The serve must be struck hard enough to clear the net yet softly enough to land in the tiny square (called the Service Box) diagonally across the court from the server. This is one of the reasons someone has put all that tape or paint on the tennis court, spoiling quantities of clay that could have been used for pottery or expanses of asphalt where you could have parked your Land Rover or Hummer.

If, as is often the case, the ball that is served should land outside the service box, it is called a Fault. If the ball lands in the net, it is called a fault. If the server steps over the baseline before striking the ball, it is called a foot fault. Finding fault is a key part of tennis and explains its popularity among married couples and families.

A served ball that strikes the net and then falls into the service box does not count but entitles the server to another serve. It is like a foul ball in baseball or a dead ball in any other sport, but is called a "Let" in tennis even though everyone can see that what got in the way was the "Net." It should also be noted that if any part of a player or a player's clothing or racquet should so much as brush the net, the point is forfeited, as if one had touched the Ark of the Covenant. This possibility provides an excellent reason for staying as far away from the net as possible. A point may also be forfeited if a ball that has already clearly sailed outside the confines of the court comes into any contact with a player or any part of a players clothing or racquet. This possibility provides an excellent reason for staying as far away from the ball as possible.

If the server faults twice in a row, that is called a double fault and the server loses the point. He or she must then trudge to the other side of the baseline and repeat the process again until enough points are lost so that the service game itself is lost and it is someone else's turn to commit fault. All day long a steady procession of anxious players dressed in sparse, ill-fitting clothes steps up to the baseline to commit and publicly acknowledge fault, as if they were penitents in some stern religious order, different from the Puritans of Increase and Cotton Mather, only in the adoption of an even more humiliating dress code.

If, as occasionally does happen, a serve should land in the proper service box, the person on that side of the court must return it before it bounces twice. Play continues in this fashion until a ball lands

Tennis, Anyone?

in the net, flies outside the lines at the end or sides of the court, or bounces more than once. In all probability, play will not continue very long before one of these events occurs. At this juncture a point has been won by one side and lost by the other. The first side to win four points wins a game; but instead of counting the points one, two, three, and four, tennis counts them as Fifteen, Thirty, Forty and Game. Many explanations for this manner of counting have been offered over the years, ranging from grade inflation at Ivy League colleges to the number of seconds it took King Louis XIV to win each point, but in truth it derives from the number of loaves of bread that Marie Antoinette used to wager on her matches. This is why Marie Antoinette said, "Let them eat cake" when she was hauled off to the Bastille after she and the Dauphine had been trounced in mixed doubles by Marat and Madame LaFarge.

The score is always announced with the server's score first in order to maximize the server's embarrassment. If the game is tied after several points, the score is announced as "Deuce," even though it was up in the forties and thirties moments before, thus tracking the movements of one's stock portfolio. When a game has reached deuce, one side or the other must win two points in a row to win the game. The player who wins the point after deuce is said to have the Advantage, and the score is given as "advantage Mr. X." Remember, Mr. X's advantage is a temporary one for tennis purposes only. Players should protest promptly if Mr. X starts taking advantage of them in any other way.

The first side to win six games wins a "Set." Unfortunately, the set that is won is only a theoretical construct, like a set in mathematics, rather than something useful, like a dinette or television set. To win a television set, you have to open a bank account, but that requires you to have some money, which you will find you have spent on tennis gear and tennis lessons.

Naturally, the rule that six games win a set has its exceptions and caveats. Even if a side has reached six games, it must have won at least two more games than the other side. In classic tennis, matches could theoretically last forever—rather than just seeming to last forever—until the requisite two game differential is achieved; sets might be won by scores such as seven to five, eleven to nine or one thousand four hundred fifty-two to one thousand four hundred and fifty, the last being numbers the players might try to claim as their SAT scores. Few players, umpires, spectators, or tennis balls could endure matches this long, however, especially on the macadam courts near sewage disposal plants where so much of your tennis is likely to be played.

Tennis accommodated these facts of modem life by adopting the tiebreaker, in which, when the score reaches "six all" (tennis speak for a score of six to six), players play a long game to determine who wins the set. There are many variations of the tiebreaker, and players often improvise their own, such as going to the bar and seeing who can drink the most beer, whiskey sours, etc. In the most frequently used tiebreaker, however, the first side to seven points wins, provided, again, that there is a two point differential. Sets can thus still theoretically last forever, and scores can still reach astronomical figures. By the logic of tennis, this change is considered progress, and revolutionary progress at that.

The rules for tennis doubles follow those of singles except that the court (like many of the players as they become older) is wider. Although there are two players on each side, only one player may strike the ball at any given time, and the other player must refrain; though not specifically prohibited by the rules of tennis, players often, though not always, also refrain from striking one another. Balls may now be considered "in" and allow play to continue if they fall within the two long rectangular boxes at the sides of the court. These boxes are called "Alleys," as in the places in cities where people are mugged, robbed, and accosted by strangers. The players on some teams spend much of their time in or near these rectangular boxes. In tennis vernacular, these players are said to be "guarding their alleys," as if the country club is on the verge of being invaded by burglars, vagrants, and litterers. The players on other teams, however, assiduously avoid the alleys in order to congregate in the middle of the court. In this position most balls are out of reach of either player, but the players find it much easier to engage in an aspect of tennis more important than any of its rules: gossiping and making snide remarks about their opponents.

Tennis, Anyone?

What the Beginner Needs to Know About the Official Code of Tennis

In addition to the rules discussed in the last chapter, the website of the United States Tennis Association contains something called "The Code—The Players' Guide for Unofficiated Matches." I will highlight here a few of the more unusual parts of the Code which seem to have been designed with unusual styles of play much like your own in mind.

Preface, line 1, deals with what happens when "your serve hits your partner stationed at the net" or when your serve "before touching the ground, hits an opponent who is standing *back* of the baseline?" Answer: According to the Code, you clearly lose the point in the first scenario, but what will happen in the real world in the second scenario is that you and your opponent will argue all day about who wins the point, making it unlikely that you will actually have to play much tennis.

Rule 37: What happens after "the Server's racket accidentally strikes the Receiver and incapacitates" him or her? Answer: Surprisingly, the Code concludes that the Server wins the match. But there is a catch: The Server loses the match by deliberately maiming a Receiver through acts such as "[h]itting a ball or throwing a racket in anger." The Code leaves much to be desired here. Who is to say what is anger and what is accident for one as clumsy as you? And what is the point of spending all that money to buy a tennis racquet if it cannot be thrown in anger on the tennis court?

Rule 33: "Talking During a Point," which is actually about not talking and includes the following two sentences:

> "A player shall not talk while the ball is moving toward the opponent's side of the court. If the player's talking interferes with an opponent's ability to play the ball, the player loses the point."

Despite the apparent certainty of the Rule, caution should be used in invoking it, especially when the gossip during a match has taken a particularly juicy turn.

Rule 35: This rule, more than any other, seems to have been particularly designed with you in mind. It warns that "a request for a let because the player tripped over the player's own hat should be denied." This rule probably explains, among other things, why Bella Abzug did not become a professional tennis player. Note for future emergencies that the rule says nothing about tripping over sun visors, headbands, bandanas, or sunglasses.

Rule 1: This is the most basic rule of all, titled "Courtesy." It proceeds on the naive and unrealistic premise that tennis should be "a fun game" in which one's opponent's good shots, rather than one's own good qualities (if any), are praised. Things go even further downhill from there because the Rule goes on to condemn the following:

"Conducting loud postmortems after points" [What's the point of a postmortem unless it's loud enough so that everyone can hear that your partner is to blame for everything?];

"Losing your temper, using vile language, throwing your racket or slamming a ball in anger" [If these activities are gone, what is left of tennis as a vehicle for exercise or physical and mental well-being?];

"Sulking when you are losing" [Who ever sulks when they are winning?].

The Rules are there on the worldwide web for browsing. But the choice to follow them or not is yours. And after you abandon the tennis website and engage in further boorish, ignorant behavior, remember that you can also go back on line to buy copies of *The Wimp's Guide to Tennis* to give by way of apology to all the people you will have offended with this behavior. That way, you'll feel no guilt about engaging in even more ignorant, even more boorish behavior. You'll feel good about yourself and so, as soon as the check clears, will the author.

Jim Kobak

A Preliminary Tennis Quiz

1. Helen Wills Moody was...
   - (a) a tennis player who married Mr. Moody;
   - (b) a tennis player who changed her name from Wills to Moody to become a member of a British rock band;
   - (c) despite her name, a cheerful person, capable of laughter.

2. The correct response to a lob is...
   - (a) to run backwards frantically, look directly into the sun, take a mighty swing and hit the ball into the bottom of the net;
   - (b) to start blowing at the ball and call it out;
   - (c) to forget about blowing at the ball and call it out anyway.

3. Doubles was invented...
   - (a) by the Marquis de Sade, as torture;
   - (b) by tennis equipment companies, so that more people could play tennis and have to buy racquets and other equipment;
   - (c) as a business development plan, by divorce and criminal defense lawyers.

4. In hitting a backhand the most important thing to remember is...
   - (a) to bend the knees, follow through, and look at the ball;
   - (b) to change the grip on the racquet;
   - (c) to yell "yours" and remind your partner to bend her knees,

Tennis, Anyone?

watch the ball, follow through, change the grip on her racquet, and pick up some butter at the grocery store after the match is over.

5. Wind can become an important factor on the tennis court because...
   (a) it blows the ball around unpredictably;
   (b) it blows the thinnest player around unpredictably;
   (c) it blows hairdos around unpredictably.

6. Pete Sampras suffered dehydration and had his tongue hang out during long tennis matches because...
   (a) even though named Pete, he was part Saint Bernard;
   (b) he happened to have been born with a long tongue;
   (c) he had a habit of eating bad Mexican food before a match.

7. "Play a let" means...
   (a) get off our court and take up some other game;
   (b) let's play the point over because we were talking so much we can't remember what happened;
   (c) I can't get away with calling yet another unreturnable serve out.

8. "Play it again, Sam" means...
   (a) your name must be Sam;
   (b) your opponent must be Humphrey Bogart;

(c) you will feel more comfortable at a place like the New York Film Festival or the Angelika Theater than on a tennis court.

9. Playing up and back refers to…
   (a) a position in the Karma Sutra;
   (b) stationing yourself as far away as possible from your partner on a tennis court;
   (c) a doubles strategy in which both players decide to play at the net but only one has the energy to get there.

10. Tennis elbow is…
    (a) a condition in which one elbows one's partner out of the way on as many points as possible;
    (b) a condition in which one nudges listeners to underscore the punch lines while recounting amusing tennis anecdotes
    (c) the uncooked macaroni you forgot to put in the oven while you were playing tennis.

11. Spinning a racquet and asking someone the question, "Rough or smooth?" is…
    (a) a grown up version of spin the bottle;
    (b) a vestigial religious rite derived from the prehistoric Aztec ball game in which losing players were given a choice of being eviscerated frontward or backwards;

Tennis, Anyone?

    (c)   not a particularly effective conversational icebreaker.

12.   A correct service motion is…
- (a)   serving from the left and clearing from the right;
- (b)   achieved once in their lifetimes by a few elect people chosen by predestination;
- (c)   better used for hailing taxicabs.

13.   Tennis racquets achieved their present dimensions and composition because…
- (a)   people actually use them most often for playing air guitar in the privacy of their own homes;
- (b)   tennis racquet manufacturers needed an excuse to sell new racquets and charge more money for them;
- (c)   they fit nicely with the tennis racquet covers that the manufacturers also sell to make even more money;
- (d)   thanks to climate change deniers, there are no more forests and therefore no more wood for wooden racquets.

14.   The proper time to change balls in a tennis match is…
- (a)   when all the balls from the start of the match have been lost;
- (b)   when the balls are so old that they have ceased to bounce and leave divots in the court, even when it is a hard court;
- (c)   when all the balls are in the mouths of golden retrievers.

Jim Kobak

The Art of Picking Up the Ball

Few movements repay practice as consistently as the technique for picking up a tennis ball. After all, other than searching for balls in nearby ponds and nettle patches, no action is repeated nearly as often as picking up a ball one has swung at and missed entirely or allowed to roll to some inconvenient place on the court. With practice, picking up these balls will come to seem almost as natural and effortless as surreptitiously tossing them into the nearby ponds and nettle patches so that there will be no more balls with which to play and the game must be discontinued.

Many beginning players simply wander off after loose, mis-hit balls and instinctively bend over to pick them up. Like any other movement on the tennis court which is natural and easy, this movement is wrong. Because of the vast number of loose, mis-hit balls that must be picked up in even a half hour of court time, this method becomes fatiguing and can lead to chronic back pain. Boris Karloff began his career as a handsome leading man. Then he installed a tennis court at his Hollywood mansion without spending the extra money to buy this book. Stooping over to pick up loose balls, he soon developed a humpback and could be cast only as Frankenstein's Monster or Quasimodo. So unless you enjoy swinging on bell ropes or being chased by Middle European peasants with pitchforks and lanterns—in which case you should be reading *The Wimp's Guide to Cross-Country*

Tennis, Anyone?

Skiing—it is wise to develop a stylish, ergonomically correct ball pickup technique.

One such technique is hitting the ball a few times with the racquet while it is on the ground so that—in theory—it bounces comfortably onto the racket. One drawback to this technique is that it requires application of a precisely calibrated amount of force. Apply too little force and the ball just sits there, much as you wish you could; apply too much force, as you will the longer the ball just sits there, and the ball will shoot off in random directions. Of course, this result isn't all bad since it so closely resembles your play and makes it impossible for observers or opponents to know when you have finished picking up the balls and when you have begun playing. Furthermore, there is an excellent chance that before too long a ball will fly straight up and hit you in the eye, rendering everything blurry, like LSD, and enabling you to use blindness as an excuse to abandon tennis and go back to being a hippie.

A classic ball pickup technique is to nudge the ball to the side of the foot, hold the ball there with the racquet, and lift the foot. This can be a particularly elegant ball pickup technique if executed with the proper nonchalance, élan, insouciance, and other sophisticated, Cole Porter-sounding words of French derivation. The technique loses much of its elegance if executed improperly or with words of a French Canadian, Tex-Mex, or Jersey Girl extraction, or if performed near a fire hydrant. Having mastered this ball pickup technique, one may wander from court to court accumulating tennis balls for later use or sale without ever having to play a game or even lifting the racquet above waist level.

For non-purists with money to burn, vacuum devices can be purchased to suck up tennis balls along with various tennis debris such as abandoned wrist bands and players who are dead, injured, or very tired. One can also unleash a pack of golden retrievers on the court, although without careful supervision the balls and several of the players may be gnawed into a state of uselessness. Finally, one can purchase a sub-machine gun from an unscrupulous small arms dealer and spend several pleasant minutes shooting at all the tennis balls one has missed with the racquet. This technique results in quizzical looks from other players, partial loss of hearing, and a probable jail term. But those drawbacks must be balanced against that rarest of feelings that this technique affords: a few moments of actual satisfaction on a tennis court.

Tennis, Anyone?

Choosing a Tennis Racquet

Perhaps no item of tennis equipment is more important than the tennis racquet, the one item of equipment that may protect you from the ball and the ire of other players. Choosing a racquet is far from a simple matter, however. Tennis racquets in a bewildering array of shapes, sizes and substances line the walls of pro shops and sporting goods stores across the United States. Every day manufacturers introduce more sophisticated versions of existing racquets with new and enhanced features, the most astounding of which is the price tag. Some of the latest additions to the field include the following:

The Vivaldi Four Seasons. Strung with nylon, this racquet provides hundreds of hours of tournament play; strung with catgut, it doubles as a viola. Frame available in wood and graphite. Manufacturer emphasizes that wood is warranted only for slow clay courts and chamber music written before 1870.

The MX Tactical Commander. Constructed completely out of silicon chips by Taiwanese systems analysts frustrated by the inability of their nation ever to advance beyond the first round of Davis Cup competitions, this revolutionary piece of equipment is considered the logical extension of the over-sized Prince racquet: it is programmed to operate by remote control, thus allowing the player to serve, volley, etc., without the inconvenience of having to run after the ball. In fact, in social doubles the players can exchange shot after shot at championship level without moving a muscle, breaking the flow of conversation, or ever having to set foot on those hot, dusty tennis courts.

For serious men's singles matches, extra racquets can be ordered secretly from the manufacturer and hidden in concrete silos beneath the court. Guided by heat sensors, these racquets search out and destroy opponent's lobs, giving you total control of the net and all of Europe west of the Rhine. Batteries extra. Instructions in Taiwanese.

The Executive String-Puller. Don't lose those brilliant insights into supply-side economics that occur to you just as your opponent tosses the ball for his serve. Special engineering allows you to dictate in mid-volley, reply to emails, and do mathematical calculations while chasing down drop shots, on a miniature, solar-powered tape recorder/computer embedded in the racquet's throat. So don't just mutter obscenities at your racquet; communicate with it as a partner in business as well as sport. For cloudy days, when solar power is undependable, the sweet spot in the center of the racquet has been designed to function as an emergency abacus.

The Spaghetti Racquet. Banned by most tennis federations but given two and a half stars by the Guide Michelin, these racquets have traditionally been custom-strung at a trattoria on the outskirts of Bologna. Specially treated strings cause tennis balls to react in unexpected ways while also adding unexpected zest to meatballs. Efforts to create an all-purpose Pasta Paddle, suitable for squash, racquet ball, and ping-pong as well as tennis, have so far foundered on a mound of uncooked spinach linguini.

The John McPhee Birch Bank Original. Only two models are known to exist of this, the only tennis racquet made entirely from natural substances. John Noah Rondeau, legendary but astigmatic hermit of the Adirondacks, produced these racquets in his first, unsuccessful attempt to create a pair of snowshoes. Watered periodically, the racquets will last as long as the hills and smell like the great outdoors. Unwatered, they attract flies and shed on the sofa. In either case, they cost as much as an oil-shale lease.

The BioTech High Point. Genetic engineering involving a sponge, three bamboo shoots and a soup tureen produced this unique blend of suppleness, strength, and ability to mop up wet spots on a tennis court.

The Trend-Maker Deep Throat. Just because you look feminine doesn't mean you have to give up tennis. The frame of the racquet is covered in stylish nine-ply denim previously worn by Anna Kournikova. The strings have been scented by Avon and color-coordinated by Ralph Lauren. As the player grows older and plays tennis less often, pieces of the mink-lined handle can be peeled of and used for other purposes such as boas, hats and gloves.

The Wimbledon Walkman. Poach from your partner while playing everything from Presley to Pavarotti. Thousands of hair-thin fibers, capable of picking up public radio and television stations around the globe, are woven into every string. Racquet emits forty watts per channel on forehand side, thirty-seven backhand, under most conditions. Buy a second racquet for your doubles partner, go up to the net together, and voila! You not only win trophies; you have a stereo rivaling one assembled from the costliest components.

The Clara Barton First-Aider. The only racquet recommended by the Red Cross and the Montclair, New Jersey, Volunteer Ambulance Unit, this beauty guarantees your safety on the court at all times. Racquet disassembles faster than you can say, "Out goes the bad air, in comes the good." Metal frame converts into a splint and forceps; grip unravels into an Ace bandage; strings may be used as emergency sutures. Racquet cover comes embossed with personal health care plan identification number and complete, do-it-yourself layman's guide to microsurgery.

Strokes

Tennis strokes fall into one of three categories: groundstrokes, used to hit balls that have hit the ground long before you could get to them; non-groundstrokes, such as serves, overheads and volleys, used to hit balls before they hit the ground, in order to prevent them from getting dirty; and different strokes for different folks, the unorthodox swings that most players actually use, derived from playing baseball, field hockey, or bass drum in a marching band.

The Forehand Groundstroke

Tennis instruction usually begins with the most natural-seeming stroke, the forehand. The forehand is natural in the sense that the Marquis de Sade's relationship with Justine could be called natural: easy for him but difficult to conceive of, let alone implement, for anyone else. And while the Marquis claimed to have done many things with or to Justine, none involved a tennis racquet.

The tennis instructor will tell you to begin by shaking hands with the racquet. (Tennis has very aristocratic origins and places a premium on politeness toward any person or object in the vicinity of a tennis court.) Then the instructor will tell you to draw your arm back. So far, so good. Things quickly take a turn for the worse, however, as the instructor will now direct a ball toward you and ask that you move your arm forward and strike the ball. At this point, panic sets in. Above all else, keep shaking hands with the racquet. Now that you have been introduced, it is your best, if not your only, friend and your only possible protection against being hit by the ball.

The instructor, lacking a Justine to torment, will keep directing balls toward you. Some of the balls you will miss entirely, some you will dribble into the net, and some you will cause to sail over every fence in sight. Meanwhile, the instructor will yell at you to follow through, as if he or she were a spouse, parent, or boss. Then the instructor will yell some more, demanding that you bend your knees. It is as if, in the middle of the Marquis' latest torture, Justine was also practicing to be knighted by the Queen of England. You will be somewhat less likely to follow these instructions than you are to be knighted by the Queen of England. The instructor will therefore keep yelling. You can take heart that he or she will eventually become hoarse and face financial ruin from having to replace all the tennis balls you have hit over distant fences.

At this point the instructor will proclaim you ready to begin playing games. This is the tennis instructor's polite way of saying you have to play with someone else and start paying for your own tennis balls. You will hit these balls over even more distant fences. Now it is you, rather than the instructor, who faces financial, to say nothing of psychological, emotional, and physical, ruin.

The Backhand Groundstroke

Soon it is time to switch from learning the forehand to learning the backhand. The racquet does not like hitting backhands any more than you do, so you no longer shake hands with it. Instead, you rotate your hand one quarter turn counter-clockwise and hold your thumb vertically along the handle. In this way you may prove that you have an opposable thumb and are not a monkey, a fact that might not be apparent from your play.

With this grip, the backhand can easily be mastered. Just think of yourself backwards. To accomplish this, pretend you are Marcel Proust writing *Remembrance of Things Past* while looking at a mirror in a cork-lined room. Then face a real mirror and stride forward while swinging your racquet backward, remembering that what you are now seeing is no longer the mirror image of Marcel Proust but rather the mirror image of the mirror image of yourself swinging a racquet backward in space but forward in time. Easy enough, like understanding black holes or solving Fermat's last theorem. Just remember not to swing the racquet too hard because it was Marcel Proust, not you, who had the cork-lined room, and if you should shatter the mirror it's a lot of work for the maid and will give you a lifetime of bad luck that you will have to write seven long novels about, in French.

Since the backhand grip is different from the forehand grip, one must remember to change grips depending on where the ball is hit and what stroke one intends to employ to stroke the ball. Panic may ensue as play grows more rapid. The line between forehand and backhand grows evermore indistinct as balls are hit harder and harder and closer and closer to valued anatomical features. Players may lose their grip on reality as well as the racquet. As the racquet falls uselessly to the court, gender confusion, political ambivalence, and unresolved issues from childhood may emerge. It is as if one had become Marcel Proust after all, except with contusions where one has been struck by the ball.

The drawbacks of the classic backhand have led many players to shift to the less artistically pure but more readily mastered, more powerful two-handed backhand. In executing this shot one does not so much shake hands with the racquet as seize it in the manner of a two-handed beer drinker with a German beer stein during Oktoberfest happy hours at the bar. Since the two-handed backhand allows more power than the classic one-handed shot, it is possible to launch tennis balls over not just one or two but many distant fences. It is a wise precaution to yell "Fore!" before beginning the stroke. It is even a wiser precaution to yell "Fore!" and take up golf.

While you are practicing groundstrokes, the instructor will impart advice in three forms: first, the Zen paradox such as hit through the ball while also hitting over it; second, the purely theoretical Platonic ideal that is totally unrealizable in practice, such as hit the ball at the top of the bounce; and third, the utopian fantasy, such as stride into the ball and stay moving on the balls of your feet. Unless you are a connoisseur of philosophy, all this advice may be safely ignored, as it has been by generations of tennis players before you.

Volleys and Overheads

Just as mankind eventually tired of always walking on the ground and invented airborne transportation, so too you may eventually tire of groundstrokes without respite and venture toward the net to strike balls while they are still in flight. Unfortunately, mankind had the Wright Brothers to invent the airplane, while all you have is a variation of a tennis racquet supposedly invented by someone like Jack Kramer or Ted Slazenger. The racquet cannot actually fly or propel you off the ground, but it can be used to waive at passing balls as they travel on toward the back of the court, much as the ground crew at the airport waives an incoming airplane to the gate, being careful always to get out of the way.

If you should inadvertently strike the ball while waiving your racquet randomly in all directions, the resulting shot is called a Volley. Volleys should be sharp, well-angled and punchy, just as my editor insists the sentences of this book should be. You will fulfill these criteria about as often as the sentences in this book satisfy my editor, which is to say about two or three times, tops. Those will indeed be moments of rapture when birds sing, flowers blossom, your soul is wafted aloft on gentle zephyrs, and you could win points as well as praise for purple prose from your long-ago English instructor.

Unfortunately, you are unlikely to be playing your long-ago English instructor, who is now probably dead, a golfer, or perhaps both. The people with whom you are playing will pounce on your volleys, not like an English instructor, but like a school principal spotting a wad of bubble gum on a desk. They will, in short, make returns that are sharper, better angled and punchier than the volleys that precede them. It is like trading epigrams with Oscar Wilde or rapping against Eminem.

Even more humiliating experiences on the tennis court are, however, possible. They are called *overheads* and *overhead smashes*. You may associate overhead with something stores have to meet, a sort of necessary evil of the business world. Stores, however, sell merchandise and employ accountants to tell them what their overhead is and how to meet it. As a tennis player, you are a purchaser of merchandise rather than a seller. At best you might have an accountant for things like your income tax, but he or she will be largely useless to you on the tennis court, and indeed will probably go to great lengths to avoid ever being on the same court with you.

The theory behind the overhead is that, by dropping your racquet back, arching your back, pointing your hand upward, squinting into the sun, and reaching blindly upwards with your racquet, you will be able to smash a ball hit way above your head with great force in whatever direction you wish. This, however, is only a theory, and it comports rather poorly with several competing and more proven theories such as gravity, inertia, and those underlying the rest of physics. While the overhead stroke will seldom result in your actually striking the ball, it is useful to engage in periodically as the swatting motion often scares away flies.

Some players confuse the *overhead* smash with the *overheard* smash. The *overheard* smash is an especially choice remark made on an adjoining court, such as those made by the women on Court 4 describing their ex-husbands' future wives or former mistresses. It is not advisable to attempt an overhead smash while simultaneously eavesdropping on an overheard smash. The head and neck muscles must move in opposing and mutually exclusive directions, and you are all too likely to pull a muscle while missing the ball or, even worse, failing to learn the juicy *denouement* of a marital crisis.

Lobs and Drop Shots

Two other shots should be mastered, but won't be. One is the Lob, executed by hitting under the ball to propel it skyward. A successful lob is one hit high enough to produce rain, allowing you to curtail the game and go home to curl up with a good book. Do not overdo the lob: you might wind up with a crick in your neck and, according to NASA, there is already too much debris in outer space.

The Dink or Drop Shot refers to a ball that drops to the court inches from the net, to the surprise of your opponent, who has spent most of the afternoon sauntering behind the base line in order to the better to watch your wayward shots sail up to, against, and over the fence. To hit the dink, make your handshake with the racquet a limp one, as if being introduced to a child or an elderly dowager.

It is also possible to hit a dink when the ball hits the frame of the racquet rather than the strings. Technically, this type of shot is referred to disparagingly as a mis-hit, but will serve you well and may enable you actually to win a point from time to time. Among its other advantages, use of the frame in this manner means that you do not have to worry about breaking the strings in your racquet as other players do. In fact, the more you play, the more mis-hits you will accumulate, keeping the strings pristine but imparting to the frame of your racquet a worn and ancient look fitting the rest of your demeanor and creating the possibility that you could unload the racquet for a tidy sum on *Antiques Road Show*.

The Serve

The serve is the most important shot in tennis since it initiates every point. It may seem easy to serve. And it is, at a cocktail party, if you have a large tray, a good caterer, and plenty of canapés. But serving on a tennis court is a different kettle of fish entirely. The tennis balls are even larger and more inedible than Swedish meatballs, the racquet is far more porous than almost any tray, and the other people on the court are not paid caterers but opponents who are too rude even to reply to your cocktail invitations.

Tennis, Anyone?

To begin serving, start with the twist serve. Pull the racquet back as if scratching your back. In fact, you might as well scratch your back while you are at it. Then twist yourself into as uncomfortable a posture as possible, throw the ball in the air, count to three, close your eyes, do the twist again like you did last summer, and swing as hard as you can at a spot where you imagine the ball to be. Now open your eyes to see that you have either missed the ball entirely or propelled it many yards past the service box, maiming an opposing player, linesperson, or innocent bystander. At this point commence your second serve.

The second serve should be a slower, less hectic version of the first. Since dances of the Fities did not seem to do the trick on the first serve, it is best to think in terms of other art forms. Closing your eyes and visualizing twentieth-century paintings should fill the bill nicely here. First, think of the tennis ball as an airborne object in a Marc Chagall mural and toss it somewhere randomly. Then recall Duchamp's *Nude Descending a Staircase* and move your body accordingly. Finally, move your racquet forward in the pattern of a Calder mobile. When you open your eyes to discover that you have not only double-faulted but felled a player on another court, think of it not as losing a point in tennis but as making a statement through performance art.

Many people serve with a Western, rather than Eastern, grip because they have moved to Sunbelt states like Arizona, California, and New Mexico and have adopted the theory that opponents on the other side of the net must be evil, replacing the Communists who used to be on the other side of the Iron Curtain. They then reason that it was a westerner, Ronald Regan, not the effete eastern snobs of mainstream liberalism who defeated Communism. This reasoning may not earn them an A in Political Science, but does give them booming first serves, the aim of which is to obliterate an Evil Empire. Unfortunately, this reasoning is short on the nuance in which the effete Eastern press specializes and leads to weak second serves.

Some players learn to apply extra spin to their serves. These serves are called kick serves. To execute them, a player must think in terms of dance, where spins and kicks of various kinds are *de rigueur*. Classic ballet, modern dance, or lively polkas will all do, depending on a player's age and body type. Be warned, however, that in cases where one has a severe tennis instructor, family member, or tennis partner, the object most likely to have been spun, kicked, and otherwise abused at the end of the day is not the ball but oneself. Special precautions are in order if any of the other people on the court is a former Rockette or Las Vegas show girl (one should be so lucky) or (more in keeping with one's usual luck and dating history) someone named Gogolak, Vinatieri or Lou "The Toe" Groza.

At this point, your basic tennis instruction is over, along with invitations to play, access to any courts, or communications about tennis with anyone but your lawyer. Now it is time to turn to the finer points of the game: these are best mastered by selling the racquet and using the proceeds to watch tennis on TV while ingesting a variety of alcoholic, hallucinogenic, and generally forbidden mood-enhancing substances.

Jim Kobak

Other Tennis Gear

One might think that the only expensive and indispensable item of tennis equipment would be the racquet. Thousands of employees of tennis equipment companies and owners of pro shops exist to prove that such thinking is wrong.

Consider the huge tennis equipment bags that tennis players lug not only to and from the tennis court but also to the supermarket, the office, the subway station, or anywhere else where they wish to be identified as tennis players. These capacious portmanteaus, often larger than the players themselves, would not come into being, posit the manufacturers and sellers of tennis equipment, unless there were a need for a great deal more tennis equipment. And the manufacturers and sellers oblige by manufacturing ever more gear that in turn leads to ever more capacious tennis bags. This is the tennis version of Q.E.D. and cogito ergo sum in philosophy, except that in tennis no one knows Latin.

Wrist bands and headbands are the most ubiquitous of many tennis accoutrements. Some players carry scores if not hundreds of these bands, even though most do not have more than two wrists or one head. The ostensible purpose of these items is to keep perspiration from seeping into a player's eyes or hands, but except during income tax audits, perspiration scarcely qualifies as a consideration for most players. Rather, the chief purpose of the bands is to intimidate other players and even passersby on the street into believing that the wearer of the band is a real tennis player in tip-top shape. The bands generally employ vivid colors to distract onlookers away from the wearer's actual shape, often a dead giveaway of a player's true conditioning.

The bag itself furthers the intimidation mystique since, for all that anyone knows, it could contain not only tennis apparel galore but also any number of machine guns or chemical and biological agents. And in fact the bag may well contain toxins more noxious than any known biological agents if, as often is the case, the tennis garments inside it have not recently been washed.

Tennis shoes are another item of tennis gear widely thought to be indispensable by all but a few barefoot, diehard Grateful Dead adherents. At one time, tennis footwear was a simple affair, consisting of plain white canvas sneakers made either by the U.S. Keds Company or, in a few cases, crafted entirely by hand by Jack Purcell, a hermit in Canada. A powerful cartel of podiatrists, thirtysomething marketing directors at clothing companies, and Michael Jordan emerged with the advent of MTV and aerobic dancing and soon brought these Edenic days to a close. Keds found its supply of canvas mysteriously cut in half and its allotment of rubber diverted to manufacture of Superballs. As for poor old Jack Purcell, he is believed to be trudging shoeless through the snow somewhere in the Yukon, his hermit's cabin now a charred remnant of suspected arson and his once shiny canvas-stretching equipment the rust-encrusted home to vultures and wolves.

Jim Kobak

Modern tennis footwear employs all kinds of revolutionary new materials, patented technology, and edgy, post-modem new graphic design. More important, it employs tens of thousands of podiatrists, tens of thousands of thirtysomething market directors, and Michael Jordan at tens of thousands of times the salary of the rest of them combined. This new footwear technology is so sophisticated that Richard Feynman shied away from describing it in any of his books, and James Watson has not even once claimed to have discovered it. Many players now require diagrams and instruction manuals simply to lace up in the locker room. Woe betide the player whose lace has broken during a match without an adequate rider to his or her insurance policy. Broken laces may in any event become a thing of the past as a worldwide cartel of footwear manufacturers and podiatrists have aggressively changed their recommendation for the timing of purchases of new tennis shoes from every year or two to every six months, to every three months, to every three weeks, to every three games.

One corollary to the increased sophistication of tennis footwear is that it can no longer be referred to as sneakers, and youngsters who persist in the forbidden terminology at tennis camps have their mouths washed out with soap (except in North Korea, where their mouths are washed out with lye). Another corollary is that purchasers are now required to adapt the inferior, outmoded design of their foot to the superior, more modem design of the shoe rather than vice versa. Thus, wearers of tennis shoes must now purchase insoles and orthotics, specially engineered tennis socks made from discarded astronaut suits, and expensive operations for removal of bunions, plantar warts, and gangrenous toes. By strange coincidence, all of these products or services are provided by the same podiatrists and equipment companies who designed the shoes.

It is interesting to observe that none of the people involved in the design and marketing of this equipment actually plays tennis. Podiatrists generally play golf at Myrtle or Pebble Beach, depending on the number of shoe companies whose products they recommend. The thirtysomething market directors take up skiing in order to destroy their feet, ankles, and knees in one fell swoop rather than through years of agony on the tennis court. And Michael Jordan has been filmed, videotaped, and photographed on basketball courts, golf courses, baseball diamonds, and many other athletic venues —but never once on a tennis court.

The price of tennis footwear varies in direct proportion to the size, marketing budget, and color of the manufacturer's logo on the side of the shoe. It was a major triumph of the marketing directors to invert the normal principles of advertising so that rather than having the manufacturer pay for the privilege of advertising its product to others, the users at whom the advertising is aimed now pay the manufacturer. That is, the more obtrusive and recognizable the logo, the more you pay. When compared to the former cost of Keds and Jack Purcells, the price points of modern tennis footwear fall into three categories: pretty steep, you must be joking, and charge it to your ex.

The same principles that apply to tennis footwear apply with equal force to other items of tennis apparel, such as tennis dresses, tennis shorts, tennis shirts, and tennis hats. These items once came in white only, with scarcely an adornment beyond a sedate alligator or barely noticeable letter W. At one time men played tennis in flannel pants, linen jackets, and Panama hats, while women were covered from neck to ankle, wore bloomers, and carried parasols as well as racquets to the court. Those days have vanished forever. Gussie Moran wore gold lame panties at Wimbledon in the 1950s, and it was only a matter of time and television ratings before flannel pants gave way to shorts, short shorts and thongs; dresses and bloomers became halter tops and bikinis; and Panama hats and parasols were forsaken for baseball hats turned backwards. Designers appeared. Colors blossomed as tennis players in the 1960s and '70s swapped equipment manufacturers, tennis partners, and spouses with abandon and embroidered their formerly drab attire like so many later day Hester Prynnes at the end of *The Scarlet Letter*.

Eventually many tennis clothes became so skimpy that players needed to invest in expensive warm-up suits to stop feeling cold and being arrested as hookers on city streets. In this way, the sport has come full cycle. Tennis players are again often fully covered from head to toe, although now they purchase more items of clothing at higher prices to achieve this state. In the process, tennis clothing has become *très*

Tennis, Anyone?

chic and even more *très* expensive. Many people now get far more use of their tennis clothes at Walmart's, dinner parties, and opera houses than they do at the tennis court, if indeed they venture to that venue at all. Ralph Lauren and the Williams sisters are even now rumored to be designing tennis outfits suitable for use as tuxedos and wedding gowns: only idle rumors, you think, but many marketing directors are building additions to their ski houses at Aspen and Serena Williams may have thrown her back out by hunching over her sewing machine on far too many humid evenings. Forewarned is forearmed. Start preparing now to get yourself the three things you will need for the tennis gear of the future: a bigger tennis bag, a bigger closet, and most of all…a bigger wallet..

Tennis Drills

According to tennis pros around the world, the secret to tennis is many hours of practice every day. Of course, these are people who make their living selling the tennis balls and racquets with which to practice and then charge you a fee to use the balls and racquet they have just sold you to practice with. A vast discrepancy exists between the amount of time tennis pros recommend be spent on arduous, repetitive tennis drills (eight and one-half hours per day at $125 an hour) and the amount of time the average player devotes to tennis drills (about one minute and twenty-five seconds annually).

One way to make practice drills more enjoyable is to focus on the word "drill." This word reminds most people of trips to the dentist, particularly for root canal work, one of the few activities more tedious, painful, and humiliating than having to practice tennis strokes that you cannot perform in the first place. You may be tired and frustrated from a morning, or even five minutes, of hitting cross-court backhands, but your mood will brighten considerably when you remember that you are using this session as an excuse for canceling your appointment with the periodontist. (Warning: do not use this visualization technique if the person you are playing is your periodontist. Visualize a trip to the proctologist that you are also avoiding instead.) The words "dentist" and "tennis," along with "tendonitis" and "al dente," all derive from the same root, a Greek word meaning your muscles and ligaments are as flaccid as undercooked pasta and produce more agony than hot sauce.

Tennis, Anyone?

As a medical aside, the root that causes root canal problems actually travels through your entire body and also causes tennis elbow, knee pain, and blisters.

One often heard recommendation is to begin every tennis session with stretching exercises and footwork drills. Many of these stretching exercises have been banned since their use by the Spanish Inquisition to wipe out the Cathars in the twelfth century, but some tennis pros of Catalonian descent insist on them, and a few masochistic Cathars continue to practice them. Most players, however, confine their stretching to stretching the truth about their tennis, professional and amorous accomplishments.

The purpose of footwork drills is to encourage players to use the slide step to move along the baseline; to employ the crossover step to reach balls hit to distant corners of the court; and to learn to run up or back as necessary. In short, the drills are designed to encourage players to move. Needless to say, this is irrelevant to most players' games and therefore these drills can be and are safely ignored. It is especially imperative that they be ignored if, because of the politics and intrigue that accompany the scheduling of most tennis games, you find yourself playing your podiatrist rather than your periodontist. In these circumstances the less attention that is placed on the feet, the better.

Some players begin every tennis session by playing mini-games in which they lightly hit the ball to one another while remaining within the confines of their respective service boxes. The idea is to ease the muscles and reflexes gradually into the rigors of movement in an actual game involving the court in its entirety. It goes without saying that easing into movement gradually is always an excellent idea—provided, of course, that movement cannot be avoided altogether. And indeed, these mini-games have much to recommend them. One need not hit the ball very hard, and one need not move very far, even to go to the net to retrieve the balls that roll there.

One would logically think that these mini-games would last forever, like the movie *Endless Summer*. Instead, they typically last for only a few excruciating minutes, like a Michael Jackson video. The explanation for this paradox is the close proximity that this exercise forces on players. It takes only a few vagrant forehands and mis-hit volleys before the players come to the realization that they thoroughly detest one another. At that point they scurry behind their respective baselines to maximize the physical space between them. Each player then spends the rest of the afternoon ignoring all the nuances of control that he or she set out to acquire in the mini-game and simply bashes the bejesus out of the ball, pretending it is the other player. This style of play yields short points, no cardiovascular benefit, and no improvement in one's game. On the other hand, it does generate considerable psychic satisfaction and is less likely to lead to legal difficulties than acting on these impulses with a gun.

Two other popular drills in which players may engage are the cross-court drill and hitting down the line. In these drills the players stand behind the baseline and attempt to aim the ball in a certain direction—diagonally in the case of the cross-court drill and straight ahead for the down the line drill. Since these drills, if executed correctly, result in the ball crossing the net and needing to be returned several times, they can quickly become fatiguing. The players therefore stand near the alleys so that they have less distance to walk to sit down, towel off, and wait for the paramedics to arrive.

It is often difficult to discern what drills the players are attempting because, to the untutored eyes of those not engaged in the drill, balls appear to veer off in random directions. Indeed, it is often the case that, when players hit several consecutive cross-court shots, they will be discovered to have been working on their down the line shots and vice versa. Most observers, and many players, do not understand that tennis balls are based on sophisticated ballistics technology and have been programmed as heat-seeking missiles that go to the warmest spot on the court no matter how they are struck. Players who do think about the ballistics of tennis balls often dispense with tennis and engage directly in duels instead.

The cross-court drill must be distinguished from the crosscut saw. The cross-cut saw is a tool helpful in felling trees, but of little use in tennis except when playing on severely overgrown, untended courts or possibly at the end of a match when the saw can be used to transform the racquet into little pieces of kindling useful for starting fires in the Antarctic, the only continent on which tennis has never been played and therefore the continent to which you should move as soon as possible after your drill. Confusing the cross-court drill with the cross-cut saw can lead to fruitless hours of arguments and misunderstandings with sales personnel in hardware stores, to say nothing of the purchase of useless lumberjack equipment.

Yet another common tennis drill involves one player staying at the baseline while the other plays net. The theory of this drill is that the baseline player will alternate between hitting to the net player's forehand and backhand, allowing the net player to practice hitting crisp, controlled volleys to the baseline player. Theoretically the players could continue in this fashion forever, but God wisely provided for the imperfection of man and also invented wind so that only a few shots are exchanged before the players walk off in rage and frustration. So has the Lord predestined the continuing availability of tennis courts for other players.

If executed perfectly, the up and back drill prepares net players to have balls hit to them at predetermined places in predetermined order, guaranteeing that they will be completely flummoxed if someone hits them two backhands in a row during an actual game. At the same time it trains baseline players to hit the ball directly to their opponents, guaranteeing that they will never hit a passing shot. In this way play is equalized, and points can be lost quickly and without having to walk too far to pick up the ball.

Tennis, Anyone?

Players sometimes vary this drill by beginning with each player on his or her respective baseline and then having them vie to charge the net the first time a ball is hit short. Be warned, however, that participating in this drill can cause the body of the player coming to net to experience exercise and rapid motion on the tennis court, almost as if the body had been placed unknowingly in a gym or health center. The shock as well as the exercise itself could prove disastrous to your health. Be sure to consult your physician before attempting this or any drill, especially if your physician specializes in prescribing rest and feel good muscle relaxants.

Jim Kobak

Getting in Shape to Play Tennis

Tennis is a game requiring agility, endurance, quick movement, strength of hand, and speed of foot. It would be folly to attempt participating in a sport with these demands without being in tip-top shape. A rational response would therefore be for you to forget all about tennis except when it is the only thing on television and take up something more appropriate to your level of conditioning, such as drinking games or reading this book and buying lots of extra copies for your friends.

Should you nevertheless persist in the idea of trying to play tennis out of sheer, mulish stubbornness, you will need to work out and get in shape. Remember that in tennis being round is considered being in shape only if you are the ball. Hence the first thing to do is to destroy every mirror in your house. While you are at it, destroy any photographic equipment as well. Now you can engage in a tennis exercise program without being reminded how hopeless it is.

A good next step is to go to an ATM and get a stack of currency. Vigorously scatter most of the currency to the four winds while jogging back home. This exercise is excellent preparation for the most ubiquitous activity in tennis: spending money. Take the few bills that remain by the time you get home and practice stretching them between your thumb and forefinger. Your grip will be strengthened, and learning to stretch your few dollars will be essential to any future you may have in tennis.

Tennis, Anyone?

Some tennis books (priced more expensively than this one and devoid of jokes) advocate hitting against a backboard. The authors of these more expensive, less witty books tend to be moonlighting carpenters or people heavily invested in plywood futures. If their books seem tedious and monotonous, think what their exercises will be like, especially when performed on a backboard in your studio apartment that permanently eclipses the view from your only window.

In order to be executed properly, many tennis strokes demand that the knees be bent, as if in supplication to the merciless gods of tennis. Unfortunately, this is not a position in which knees are accustomed to find themselves, either by nature or usage. Therefore practice in appeasing the gods is in order, in the form of several thousand deep knee bends a day. Few movements can rival the deep knee bend in pain, awkwardness, and tedium; thus, few movements can rival it as an introduction to tennis. Whether the gods of tennis will actually be appeased is unlikely, no matter how submissively one bends one's knees and inflicts punishment on oneself. To appease the tennis gods properly, one would also have to sacrifice at least one child or family member to a lifetime regimen of tennis clinics, tennis camps, tennis coaches, tennis academies, tennis adult education courses, and tennis retirement communities, all run by Nick Bolliteri.

Many pundits advise running wind sprints, but this particular piece of punditry is a canard that never should have escaped the editor's pen. The only people capable of sprinting in any circumstances, let alone with a breath of wind remaining in their bodies, are those in some semblance of fitness to begin with. These people might as well skip past tennis altogether and go directly to cross-country skiing, Iron Man competitions and walking the Appalachian Trail barefoot. What sense is recommending wind sprints to someone who cannot fully inflate a single balloon at a child's birthday party? In fact, as far as you are concerned, a short wind sprint from the net to the baseline might as well be the original Marathon, in which the runner said something unintelligible in ancient Greek and dropped dead at the end of the run. Rather than running wind sprints, try saying something unintelligible in modern Greek and lighting up a few cigarettes in a Greek taverna to simulate the feeling of being totally out of breath. Even better, forsake the sprint for the Sprint telephone service, and speak into the phone as distinctly as possible to cancel all tennis-related engagements for the next decade and book a flight to Crete or Santorini.

  Dance exercises have much to recommend them. After all, dancers typically have lithe, agile bodies, and their lithe, agile muscles have memories of lithe, agile, and wholly unnatural body movements that would come in handy in tennis. Dancers, of course, are always in their toe shoes at the barre and have little use for tennis shoes and tennis courts. You, too, should spend considerable time at the type of bar where you are most comfortable.

  The optimal method for incorporating dance routines into your tennis preparation regime is to eschew any use of the tennis courts at

Tennis, Anyone?

your local country club during weekend afternoons and instead go to the clubhouse building and use the time to crash as many weddings and bar mitzvahs as possible. Hydration and nutrition are constant concerns in tennis, so fortify yourself with a few drinks and several trips to the buffet tables. Then head to the dance floor and give it your all while practicing neglected dance steps from the 1950s and '60s. Strengthen your arms with the Fish and Watusi, flex your knees with the Twist and the rumba, and work the abs and torso with the Mambo, the Stroll, and the cha-cha-cha. Do not worry yourself with the type of dance music actually played by the DJ ("Brown-Eyed Girl" and the complete bootlegged works of Barry Manilow). Few, if any, other people on the dance floor will be paying any attention to the music, and if you react late, feel out of step, and stumble over someone's feet and then crash into his or her behind, just think of it as practice for doubles.

As your muscles and singing voice warm up, partake of ever faster, more vigorous exercises such as the Bunny Hop, the Hokey Pokey, the Macarena and the YMCA song. Then work up your heart rate with a polka or "Bahad Navillah," checking first to see whether you crashed a Polish wedding or a bar mitzvah. Who knows? You might get to kiss the bride or the person being bar mitzvahed. Be sure to make a few toasts (excellent practice in raising the arms for the ball toss). Then towel off with a napkin, strengthen your wrists by brandishing a steak knife or two to ward off the father of the bride, and do some quick weight and dexterity training by picking up and pocketing any potentially valuable items in the cloak room. You can cool down by jogging into the nearest woods or unlighted alley while the last bars of "Sentimental Journey" and the screams of the mother of the bride waft across the empty tennis courts.

One thinking of taking up tennis may also prepare by indulging in vigorous winter sports like hot dog skiing and Ice Capades. These sports have much to recommend them. For one thing, other than yourself, they do not involve a ball or anything that rolls, bounces, or is likely to be struck by something in the shape of a paddle. For another, they are practiced at a time of the year when ice and snow cover the lines on tennis courts and blizzards make it impossible to see the ball to call it out. Moreover, with any luck at all, these activities will leave you permanently bedridden or at least on crutches for several tennis seasons. Remember that to prepare for these activities properly, it would be prudent to purchase several copies of the author's companion book, *The Wimp's Guide to Cross-Country Skiing*. This book should afford you at least twenty minutes of enjoyment, or roughly as much as you are likely to derive from a lifetime of tennis—and at much greater profit to the author.

Finally, one can always confine one's physical activity to mealtimes and eat one's way into shape on a variation of the Atkins Diet known as the Ad In Diet. On this diet one may eat meat balls, cheese balls, melon balls, even matzoth balls and, if one is so inclined, fur balls, provided that one does so in quantities of fifteen, thirty, or forty and washes them down with Gatorade. Some people become ill, disoriented, and irritable on this diet, mirroring their feelings on the tennis court. A few find the diet fun, fulfilling, and even tasty. They become tennis umpires and lines people.

Jim Kobak

A Tennis Villanelle

After all that work getting in shape, we all deserve a respite. So here's a little poem to give you a breather and help put everything in a more refined perspective. If you are into meditation, you could use it as a chant and pretend your tennis racket is a mandala.

Tennis Villanelle 1

The years of lessons flee as soon as play begins.
"Nice get," they say. But still they call it out.
One more long day of sets we will not win.

For us embarrassment, dismay, chagrin.
Across the net high five displays and shouts.
The years of lessons flee as soon as play begins.

The backhand falls away; can't handle spin.
"Nice game," they say. But really it's a rout.
One more long day of sets we will not win.

I fail to guard my alley, cardinal sin.
A scowling partner looks away and pouts.
The years of lessons flee as soon as play begins.

Tennis, Anyone?

Flat-footed forehands seldom falling in
And feeble lobs fall prey to brutish louts.
One more long day of sets we will not win.

My opponents act like they won Wimbledon.
"Let's play again," they lie on their way out.
The years of lessons flee as soon as play begins.
One more long day of sets we will not win.

Jim Kobak

Meet the Backboard: Your Tennis Bestie

In this chapter I will reveal a little known secret that more than justifies to any sensible person the price of the book and the time spent reading this far in it. This is the technique I have discovered for reducing the risk of athletic disaster in general, and of misbegotten adventures with a tennis ball in particular. It is to confine one's athletic endeavors to playing tennis against backboards. To be sure, one may be rendered temporarily *hors de combat* by rebounding tennis balls that strike one's midsection as one glances furtively at some other player also using the backboard, and I've learned that it is possible to lose a whole can of fuchsia Spaldings in the course of one twenty-minute session with a backboard located at the apex of a steep hill. But this is as close as one is likely to come to real disaster—provided that one is not then foolish enough to think that having hit balls against a large, inanimate, stationary, and vertical slab of wood will be of any help should one venture onto the horizontal slab of an actual tennis court that will be found to contain many opponents who will not only vary in size but are likely to become quite animated once they commence play with you.

Playing against a backboard was recommended to me by a conscientious tennis pro on the verge of a nervous breakdown after three and one-half years of constant lessons and incessant exhortation had succeeded in teaching me the difference between rough and smooth

Tennis, Anyone?

and how to shake hands with the racquet. In fact, the lessons terminated abruptly one afternoon when, after ten minutes of stalled forehand drives and misfiring volleys, the tennis pro flung his racquet heavenward (or about as high as my last attempt to hit a flat backhand) and began asking himself why he had not become a stockbroker.

So I was relegated to the backboard. At first I was crestfallen. Not only could I not ride the bench of the lowliest team, I could not even cling to the lowest rung of the Tennis Ladder. But three or four satisfying thwacks against widely dispersed points on the surface of the backboard and a backhand which crashed into the surrounding chicken wire with real *éclat* turned my chagrin to joy. Here was my niche, here my perfect opponent. And so it will be for you if you follow my example. After all, if the board is squat, rectangular, and immobile, why, so are we; if we cannot serve, why, neither can it. The board does not look embarrassed when our backhands dribble up to its imaginary net; the board does not blaspheme and sputter when battered Tretorns float over it. Instead, the board greets grounders, popups, foul tips and misses with the same discreet silence. And each time we hit a good shot, we are rewarded with one of those satisfying thwacks.

You should now begin working out against the backboard faithfully. It will soon become a habit, if not an obsession, and very nearly consign to oblivion all other passions. (In my case, this was chiefly a young lady named Albertine who scarcely returned my advances with a civil word, let alone a satisfying thwack, and eventually ran off to live with Marcel, but that's a story for another book.) Indeed, next time you are at a place like an art museum facing a large color field painting bisected by a horizontal stripe, you will find yourself unconsciously drawing back your right arm, tightening your fist around an imaginary racquet handle and striding forward with your left foot.

Will all this diligence pay off? In a sense, yes. You will have developed genuinely stylish strokes. Your backhand, previously thought appropriate for an overworked lumberjack, now seems as swift as Achilles' sword. You keep your eye on the ball, bend your knees as if in a church, and execute an elegant follow-through at the slightest provocation.

You might think these finely honed strokes and accomplished mannerisms would evolve into a formidable tennis game. This is not only mistaken. It is the height of folly. The elegant strokes remain good for one thing, and one thing only: hitting tennis balls against a backboard. In a game of tennis they are worthless.

Within moments of the commencement of a set, your strokes will have deteriorated to the point where they might be mistaken for efforts to swat flies or wave flags at a Republican convention. In fact, all that having elegant strokes will do for you on an actual tennis court is get you into games that are over your head. These are any games that involve opponents between the ages of thirteen and eighty-nine who own their own tennis rackets and do not associate the American Twist exclusively with Chubby Checker, pretzels or the end of O. Henry short stories.

Consider that most essential feature of an actual tennis match, the serve. You offer up to a backboard a serve at a measured speed that will guarantee it will be returned at the time and place of your choosing, like ordering from Amazon. But your opponents are more likely to be actual Amazons rather than Amazon drivers, or even UPS drivers or U.S. Postal Service workers. They will pounce on your slow moving deliveries and gleefully rifle forehands and backhands to points that you will only reach moments or perhaps minutes after the ball is past. By this time, however, it scarcely matters, for your own serve will undoubtedly have begun to "act up," a euphemism signifying it is taking vagrant flights that terminate dead center in the wrong service box, as pathetic as a misaddressed envelope at Christmas time. Other players have bad knees and tennis elbows and even drinking problems that act up on occasion, but serves are more or less consistent.

Almost certainly your opponent's serve will not "act up." At least, it is beset by none of the vagaries that likely beset your convoluted overhead delivery. Your opponent probably does not flourish his racket above his head as if conducting the overture to the third act of *Lohengrin*. Your opponent probably does not even groan as if he had been asked to attend the third act of *Lohengrin*. For all you know, your opponent may have spent so much time polishing his serve that he is not even aware that there is a third act to *Lohengrin*.

But your opponent almost certainly will have a polished serve. One effortless flick of his wrist, and the ball is traveling toward you at the speed of light. No sooner have you reached the period for rebuttal in your internal debate about whether to take it on the forehand or backhand side than the ball has bounded past you and is about to arrive with a disconcerting clang at the base of a stoutly anchored metal fence.

So it goes for serve after serve. Should your opponent occasionally miss his first serve, he employs a second that is possessed of a demonic lateral movement that a crab would covet. You make a belated lunge to the right, and the ball skips to the left; you lean to the left, and the ball leans to the right. You do nothing, and the ball stands up, sits down and fights, fights, fights. Before the day is done, the fence has taken quite a beating. Not one satisfying thwack is heard to emanate from your side of the net, but only a steady succession of clangs such as might be heard at a cymbal-testing factory.

Until you can get back to the safety of an inanimate backboard, everything after the first game with a real person should be approached with the attitude of a Carthaginian at the conclusion of the Third Punic War: wishing you were someplace else. Rub your right calf and wince frequently, as if your failure to cover the court like a throw rug, let alone a blanket, is attributable to an old pole-vaulting injury. Adopt a look of ennui for running under lobs. Glance heavenward periodically as if the high incidence of netted backhand volleys could only be explained by reference to the possibility of Divine Intervention. You now gaze with disgust at your racquet, with which you must continue to shake hands, but only from a sense of duty.

The end comes with a drop volley: the opponent does the volleying, no doubt wishing he had a musket; you do the dropping. The score, as usual: 6-1, 6-0. Your opponent does not heave his racquet into the sky, beam radiantly, swill champagne or pay homage to his tennis coach. He does not even hop over the net

"Nice game," you say, lying through your teeth.

"I enjoyed it," replies your opponent, lying through his teeth. "It's too bad your serve was acting up," he adds condescendingly, in an attempt at *noblesse oblige*.

"We'll have to try it again sometime," you say, envisioning your opponent's next bout with a new Covid variant as a propitious moment.

There is no reply from the opponent, who is striding off the court at a brisk pace. There are limits to what your opponent will endure for the sake of *noblesse oblige*.

"You really should take in the third act of *Lohengrin*," you may call after him.

But again there is no reply. The opponent has already stalked out of earshot. Make no attempt to follow him. Who cares if he hears the third act of *Lohengrin* or not? You have three fuchsia Spaldings and a tennis racket. Now all you need is a backboard on which to lavish some *noblesse oblige* of your own.

Jim Kobak

Tennis Strategy

There are many different strategies for playing tennis. Most may be safely ignored because they are based on the fallacy that you should move to the ball rather than vice versa.

It may help to visualize tennis as a chess game. Some players are capable of moving great distances, like a queen or a castle, while others may dart about cleverly, like knights. You, however, should visualize yourself as a king. This requires other players to be suitably deferential to you and means that you may well not have to move at all for much of the game. Before you do have to move, the person who strikes the ball in your direction must first warn you by calling out, "Check;" and, even then, your movement will be confined to one step at a time. Moreover, you can claim technically not to have lost a game or even a point until someone actually comes across the net and captures you—something most players feel uncomfortable about doing.

Changing the rules of the sport as play proceeds can also prove an interesting, effective strategy. Thus, you can decide to call balls that hit the line "Out" on your side of the court and "In" on the other; claim that you get two bounces and your opponent none in any month with an "R" in it; and play a let whenever you lose a point on the grounds that you were hearing voices as a result of having stopped your medication that morning. Even with these strategies, that old standby adage "When in doubt, call it out" can always come in handy.

Combining these tactics not only evens up the play and unnerves opponents who are much better than you are, but also guarantees that you will never be invited to play with such opponents again.

One must also not overlook use of the feigned medical emergency at critical junctures of a match. When employing this tactic, one strikes the ball and then immediately makes a loud gurgling noise and writhes about in the doubles alley, as if stricken by a stroke, heart attack, or epileptic fit. (It is best to consult the medical journals for a full repertoire of trendy, catastrophic maladies as the same one seldom works more than once or twice on a given opponent.) Most other players will gasp, stand in stupefaction, or run to your aid. At this point the ball that you have hit should land untouched on the other side of the court. You may now pick yourself up, dust yourself off, and claim the point as your own. Many opponents will remain standing in stupefaction for at least several more points, which you should therefore also win easily. All other players will soon stomp off the court, allowing you to declare the match forfeited. The drawback to this technique is the occasional hot-headed player who may try to inflict on you an even worse medical condition than the one you have feigned.

Effective doubles strategy is a complicated subject requiring advanced degrees in physics, physical education, psychotherapy, and the diplomatic history of Prussia. If you lack these prerequisites, it is best to find a strong partner, make yourself as amiable as possible to him or her, glower from time to time at everyone else, and stay out of the way. Many successful doubles teams hit the ball to the middle of the opponents' court as often as possible, on the theory that the opponents are likely to be experiencing marital difficulties and will go to great lengths to avoid proximity to one another. Other teams concentrate on hitting the ball as hard as possible at the weaker player on the other team, meaning, in your case, you. One comforting thought to keep in mind in these circumstances is the rule that the fewer balls you hit back, the sooner the ordeal will be over.

It is sometimes said that a good doubles team always moves in tandem, as if on a string. Remember that this is just a metaphor. Actually tethering yourself to your partner can lead to terribly tangled ropes, terribly tangled personal relationships, and terribly tangled divorce court property settlements, to say nothing of difficulties in showering—in short, an experience much like sailing.

Other useful tactics can be learned from the history of Roman warfare. Consider the Fabian strategy of delay, named after a Roman general who delayed and delayed whenever the Carthaginians wanted to attack until they exhausted themselves and their resources and sailed back home. Fabian never won, but he never lost a battle either. He had many pillars erected in his honor and was even invited to sing "I'm a Tiger" on the *Dick Clark Show*. You, too, can avoid losing at tennis if you find enough excuses to postpone playing. Inventing and elaborating on ailments in seldom mentioned body parts, plumbing emergencies, and domestic crises will usually do the trick. You might even win some tournaments at resorts and the like if you put off your matches until everyone else has gone home and you are the only player left in the tournament.

You can also learn a trick or two from Hannibal. If he could get elephants loaded with military impedimenta over the Alps, surely you can coax a behemoth with a racquet onto a tennis court. Few sights are as formidable to an opponent as that of an untamed elephant across the net. Moreover, turning the elephant sideways at the net leaves precious little room for your opponent to hit a ball without hitting the elephant. If your opponent hits the elephant with the ball, not only is the ball likely to rebound back into the opponent's court with little effort on your part, but your opponent will in all probability be crushed to death by an angry elephant, leading to a short and certain victory. To be sure, you may have to spend a little extra time sweeping the court and could hear one or two more elephant jokes than usual at the country club dinner dance, but these surely are but small prices to pay for the thrill of decisive, not soon forgotten success on the court.

Finally, back to Fabian tactics. If nothing else works, try singing "I'm a Tiger" as loudly as your lungs allow every time you step on a tennis court.

Jim Kobak

Variety: The Spice of Life and Racquet Sports

Now that you have learned a few tennis basics, a word should be said about other racquet sports and their similarities to and differences from tennis. Otherwise, stepping onto an unfamiliar court could be fraught with danger. It is a serious faux pas to act in the way you would on a tennis court if you are in fact on a volleyball court or lacrosse field. Your behavior will be inappropriate. Your dress and gear will be inappropriate. And your attempts to find out the score will be met with ridicule. It is like being a character in a Kafka novella or ordering steak tartar at a vegan restaurant.

Probably the oldest tennis-like sport is badminton. But badminton, as it is so often played in the United States, is to modern day tennis as a tricycle is to an e-bike. The game is often played for fun at family gatherings, instantly distinguishing it from a blood sport like tennis. The goal is to hit a fluttering object called a shuttlecock over a high net. No bounces are allowed in badminton. There are not even any cheerleaders, and if there were, even they would not be allowed to bounce up and down with any enthusiasm. Badminton is an aerial endeavor like Circque du Soleil rather than an earthbound enterprise like tennis or a plain, ordinary circus. Badminton players serve upward and follow the flights of birdies while tennis players hit downward and focus on court surfaces and groundstrokes.

Tennis, Anyone?

Badminton originated in the nineteenth century in India where it was also called battledore, shuttlecock, and Poonah—names more suitable for a Harry Potter movie than a serious sport. It received its name by association with the Badminton House of the Duke of Beaufort, although it is not known whether any Duke of Beaufort actually played badminton, built a badminton court on his grounds or even owned a badminton racket. The first Duke of Beaufort, John of Gaunt, does not so much as touch a birdie or even lace up a pair of sneakers in the Shakespeare play in which he appears, so Shakespeare killed him off and focused on other characters.

Badminton has become an Olympic sport and is played seriously in much of Asia. So all you casual North American dilettantes who regard it as a relaxing diversion, beware. The feathery appearance and name of the shuttlecock belie its darker side. Badminton play at the highest level rewards deception, like the modern day Republican Party. And the harmless-looking shuttlecock is itself no innocent birdie but a lethal missile, capable of inflicting damage on real birds and other creatures. The highest recorded speed of a shuttlecock struck by a racket exceeds that of tennis ball by nearly a hundred miles an hour. Badminton players may don Jack Purcell sneakers and preppy attire, but they are killers and drone masters at heart.

Speaking of preppies leads to discussion of squash: the sport, rather than the plant, as this is a sports book not a cook book. Squash originated at Harrow, the British boarding school, in the nineteenth century through the efforts of schoolboys who should have been conjugating verbs, translating their Homer and Virgil, and otherwise preparing to become future Princes of Wales and kings of England. Instead, they prepared by hitting rubber balls against a courtyard wall where they made a squishy sound, allowing them to think they were launching sneak attacks on Dauphins of France and ruining their crème brûlées. It is not known how the "squish" sound of this original pastime was transmuted into the name "squash," which emerged from it, though early records from Harrow show generally poor attendance at spelling class.

Squash is now played completely indoors in a rather sterile and confined space where, unlike tennis, the players may hit the ball against the walls and, if they are not careful, hurtle it into them themselves. It is not a pursuit for the claustrophobic. Squash has a scoring system at least as bizarre as tennis' though quite different. In fact, squash has several different systems, including a classic hand-in-hand system derived from the practice at Harrow whereby some of the more academically adept scholarship students would write and hand in papers for wealthier students in the line of succession to the throne. Then they would hold their hands out for a tip or written promise that they would be appointed Privy Councilor or Chancellor of the Exchequer. This leads to the type of college admissions policy that a majority of the current Supreme Court believes is appropriate for educations of higher learning in a democracy rather than one that factors in diversity and leads to equality of opportunity.

Squash is a vigorous, aerobic game and, since it is played inside a small box by players who are constantly in motion, the risks of collision are omnipresent. It is not a game for the unfit or faint of heart. It is emblematic of the spirit of squash that the Titanic had a specially designed squash court on which people were playing when the ship hit the iceberg. Despite its special design, the squash court, like the rest of the boat, still sank, though in the true spirit of squash devotees the players are said scarcely to have noticed as they played on underwater.

Racquetball is another vigorous indoor sport where the ball can be hit almost anywhere. Unlike the squish from which squash emerged, the iconic racquetball shot is the splat. Another shot is called the plinth, like a building block or the thing under a statute in museums. Players may sometimes employ something called the Z-stroke. It is as if all the schoolboys at Harrow started playing squash after dropping acid.

Handball combines elements of both racquetball and squash and can be played either indoors or outdoors. It does not allow use of anything but hands to hit the ball—no racquets, paddles, whips, or implements of torture other than the nature of the game itself. Another game that may be considered a variant of squash is jai alai. A poor translation of the rules of the game into Spanish by an exchange student at Harrow not only resulted in a grade of C- but a belief that the game required use of gourds. This has led to the substitution of an elongated, tuber-like invention called the *cesta* for the racquet. Basque separatists refined jai alai until it became a source of injury for many experienced and expert players. They also devised elaborate rules and opportunities for wagers in which fortunes may be lost in the time it takes a single *pelota* to carom off a *fonton*. For these reasons, jai alai means "merry festival" in the Basque language.

A more recent addition to the menu of racquet sports is paddle tennis. (Some will quibble about the inclusion of sports played with paddles, or for that matter hands or cestas rather than racquets, in a book about tennis and other racquet sports, but I am an inclusive sort of person, and this is not the place to split hairs. That will occur when some enterprising soul writes *The Wimp's Guide to Barbering*.)

There are actually two forms of paddle tennis. The first is a version invented early in the twentieth century to conform to the topography of someone's backyard in the forested northeastern part of the United States which, like so much else, soon migrated westward. The second version was invented by someone who stayed put in Scarsdale, NY, in the 1930s. In the western version, sometimes abbreviated POP, the court is sensibly laid on the ground, even over fault zones in areas around Los Angeles, like Venice Beach or Santa Monica, where play may be interrupted not only by earthquakes but passing skateboarders and body builders and the occasional surfer who has caught a really big wave.

Tennis, Anyone?

The eastern version, by contrast, is played on a raised platform because the lot on Fox Meadow Road in the Scarsdale location where this version was invented was strewn with rocks in a manner that residents of that area (including, incidentally, the author's maternal grandparents, longtime residents of Fox Meadow Road) considered picturesque. The raised platform caught on in the northeast because it allowed for easier snow removal and could be heated on the bottom for play during the long, dreary mid-Atlantic winter; it also expressed visually the status of the elite descendants of robber barons who lived in places like Scarsdale (other than the author's grandparents whose progenitors, unfortunately, were simply robbers). Since scraping snow and ice off the court is one of its most enjoyable features, this eastern version of paddle tennis is principally played during blizzards and polar vortexes when players can neither see the ball most of the time nor move their frostbitten arms and legs to hit it on the few occasions when it is visible. Play in these conditions does, however, afford players an opportunity to bundle up in their old boarding school letter sweaters, faux Burberry scarves with matching ear muffs and freshmen beanies.

One defining feature of platform tennis, other than the platform, is the wire which surrounds the court. The original impetus for the wire was the tendency (to which I am sure most readers can easily relate) of players to hit stray balls that flew off the platform. These balls sometimes rolled into the mouths of the eponymous foxes of Fox Meadow Road where a player seeking to retrieve them courted injury

Jim Kobak

or death by rabies. At other times the balls might roll onto the road itself, where a player seeking to retrieve a ball courted injury or death from careless drivers of speeding roadsters such as Jay Gatsby, Bonnie and Clyde, or my talkative and often distracted grandmother. With the court encased in metal wire, balls fly out of it and onto Fox Meadow Road much less frequently so that players now court death or injury chiefly from frostbite or slipping on the snow and ice they failed to remove completely.

In the eastern version of racquetball, balls that hit the wires may still be in play, and proficiency in returning those balls is a key element of racquetball, almost as important an element as having several credit cards for buying all the clothing to stay warm during play. In the western version, avoiding freezing to death is less of a concern, and while California and other areas out West are sometimes considered off the wall in many ways (at least by people in Scarsdale), being allowed to hit a ball off the equivalent of a wall in paddle tennis is not one of them. In the eastern or platform version of the sport, the server is allotted only one attempt to serve per point, undoubtedly so points will be shorter and people can get to the warming shed sooner. In the western version of the game, hey, we're talking California and Burning Man and Portland, Oregon, and sometimes the server gets one serve and at other times two and people are pretty chill about it.

And now we get to pickle ball, the most recent and condensed form of racket sport, a sort of *Reader's Digest* version of tennis. For one thing, the court looks more or less like a tennis court, but is much smaller, minimizing the need for movement and also conserving space requirements; already thousands of brightly colored pickle ball courts are proliferating atop the foundations of forlorn, abandoned tennis courts, much as new civilizations build their cities on the remnants of the towns and cities they conquer, except that in this case the new structures look like Mondrians covering up the landscapes of minor post-Impressionist painters that haven't been cleaned in a long time rather than cathedrals built on the foundations of pagan temples. Because pickle ball courts are smaller than tennis courts, their numbers increase even more rapidly than the numbers of tennis courts decline, conferring evolutionary advantages that already threaten to render tennis courts, tennis players, and even tennis coaches, trainers, hangers on, and groupies endangered species. Even Brad Gilbert and Pam Shriver may become endangered species, subject to the same special protections as sea turtles and snail darters, respectively. But this does not mean that pickle ball is not trendy. Far from it. The size and ease of installation of pickle ball courts comport well with the popularity of tiny houses and small portion menus at the chic restaurants.

Aside from a few peculiarities which we will address in a moment, pickle ball is easy to play at basic level, although true proficiency has been attained by only a handful of Zen masters. Pickle ball is nothing if not noisy and brash, and boldly holds itself out as a racquet sport, yet the implement wielded in play gives every appearance of being a paddle rather than a racquet. The paddle is, though, lighter and smaller than most other paddles. So don't think you can make do by bringing an old kayak or canoe paddle to the new pickle ball court. You can, however, compensate and make do quite nicely by bringing old whiffle balls since that is the ball used in the game. The ball does not have to be replaced every few games, as at Roland Garros and Wimbledon, and does not hurt as much when it hits you as a squash ball or jai alai pelota. Contrary to popular belief, the ball is not shaped like a pickle, nor should it ever be referred to as a pickle. Pickles was the name of a dog that chased after the balls when pickle ball was first invented. It is not mandatory to bring a dog to most pickle ball courts—indeed, it is strongly discouraged by most venues for fear that the dog will gnaw on the ball or the legs of slower-moving players. But if you do bring a dog, it must at least answer to the name "Pickles." It is also not mandatory to bring a plate of pickles for other players to munch on, which can lead to messy food fights and significant brine removal expense.

  Now for some of pickle ball's peculiarities. The server gets one serve per point, and it must be an underhanded serve. Yes, that is right. This is one sport where it pays to be as underhanded as possible. The hands must not stray above the waistline until after the ball is struck. (It is sort of like dancing school in this respect, but without the white gloves.) After the serve is returned (if it is returned) the server and server's partner (if there is one) must let the ball bounce before striking it again. Players, no matter how hungry, cannot place themselves permanently in an area known as "the kitchen," thus belying the old adage, "No matter where I serve my guests, it seems they like my kitchen best," an adage favored by certain Scarsdale grandmothers who in fact left most kitchen matters to the cook and the maid. Points can only be accumulated by the team that is serving. Should this happen the score is then announced as a confused series of numbers reminiscent of an internet password but without the capital letters or special characters (unless one counts the muttered profanities added in some hotly contested matches). The game finally ends when one side has amassed an agreed upon number of points and at least two more than the other team, should anyone be able to determine whether that has occurred. It may not matter, however, because long before this, the famished players so long banished from the kitchen will forfeit or concede to a draw and repair to the sidelines to eat condiments. Particularly if they are pickle-free condiments.

Jim Kobak

The Racquet Sport Intelligence Test

Here is a test to determine your racquet sport IQ and whether you could pass the Harrow entrance exam to be eligible for its squash club.

TRUE or FALSE:

1. People were playing squash on the Titanic when it was hit by an iceberg
2. People on the Titanic's squash courts, like the band in the Titanic's ballroom, played on after the ship was hit by the iceberg and while it was sinking, at least in the movie
3. There is a causal connection between the presence of a squash court on a boat and the likelihood that it will sink

A. Which of the following statements most correctly describes why the Earl of Sandwich visits the Duke of Beaufort at Badminton House:
   1. To bring lunch
   2. To try to find and then use the badminton court
   3. To fight a duel

B. Throw a pumpkin up in the air and it comes down
   1. Squash
   2. Looking more like a pickle than a squash
   3. On the paddle tennis court

D. Which of the following does not have a net?
   1. A handball court
   2. A squash court

Tennis, Anyone?

      3. A very proficient or very dumb aerialist in Cirque du Soleil

C. Paddle tennis is sometimes called platform tennis because
      1. It is played by Republicans desperately seeking a platform because their political party no longer has one
      2. It is almost as painful to play as it is to wear platform shoes
      3. Calling it that makes it seem as if the people playing it are doing something vaguely important rather than wasting time

F. An activity in which participants bring paddles into a cage and use terms like "squish," "rough or smooth" and "mixed doubles round robin" is
      1. Racquetball
      2. Platform tennis
      3. Unlicensed sex therapy

G. Rank the following sports in order by the amount of vigorous exercise and aerobic benefit each confers:
      1. Tennis
      2. Squash
      3. Badminton

Now rank the same three sports in terms of the square footage of the court. Take the sum of the rankings for each sport and calculate their average. (Warning; This involves use of division.)

Multiply the average for each sport by the cost of the racquet needed to play it. (Further Warning: this step requires knowing your multiplication tables or owning a calculator.)

Take the number you have calculated for each sport and write it down on a piece of paper, remembering to check your work carefully. Be sure no one sees the paper. Now eat the piece of paper and proceed to question H.

H. By completing the steps in Question G, you have
   1. Procrastinated long enough to avoid playing any of the three sports for another day;
   2. Proved that you could probably pass second grade;
   3. Shown a high propensity for becoming a CIA operative;
   4. Come up with one or more new internet passwords

I. A tennis ladder is
   1. Something that with care and patience you can learn how to climb to become a tennis umpire;
   2. Bad luck if you walk under it;
   3. Even worse luck to find your name added to on the very lowest rung down near the bottom

J. Match each person in Column 1 with at least one item from the list of the people, places and things in column 2.

Column 1	Column 2
Rodger Federer	Grunting
Steffi Graff	Envy
Billy Jean King	Gluttony
Jack Karmer	Sloth
Illie Nastase	Greed
Brad Gilbert	The Warped wooden tennis rackets in the garage
Co Co Grauff	Ego
Rod Laver	Super Ego
Bill Tilden	Rolex watches
Novak Djokovic	Global Warming
Rafael Nadal	The 1960's
Susanne Lenglen	Dante's Inferno
Bud Collins	The USTA

Tennis, Anyone?

K. In three hundred words or less, after signing an affidavit that you are neither using nor do you yourself consist of artificial intelligence, compose an essay on one of the following two themes:
  1. Compare and contrast the concept of the "kitchen" in pickle ball with that of "no man's land" in tennis.
  2. Describe how the demilitarized zone between North and South Korea and the likelihood of nuclear war relates to the narrow area between you and your opponent on a squash court and the likelihood of bruises and bad feelings.

Jim Kobak

A Short Poetry Break

Since you probably failed the racquet sport IQ test abysmally you need to focus on tennis for the time being and not become distracted by the nuances and tangled relationships of its extended family of sister, cousin, niece, nephew, and bastard offspring racquet sports. To help further, the following poem, once memorized, will serve as a mnemonic device that will help you ace the next test and keep the tennis basics at the front of your mind every time you step on a court. I call it "Doubles" because (and here's a hint that might come in handy on future quizzes) that's how many lines there are when you count up all the lines for singles and doubles play on both sides of a standard tennis court.

From to to fro
The ball will go
Both back and forth
Across the court.

First there, then here,
From dark to light;
In sun, in shade,
Long points are played.
The yellow sphere,
Always in flight.

Tennis, Anyone?

The game defined
By fourteen lines,
Which both confine
And give design.

Jim Kobak

Tennis and Culture: The Sociology of Tennis

Despite a growing aversion to goose liver pate, a group of enterprising cultural anthropologists recently concluded a decades-long study of American dining customs. The data collected by the anthropologists spell out a fascinating pattern: the rules for successful dinner party conversation conform almost exactly to the rules for effective doubles strategy in tennis. (The study was actually performed by living among the residents of Bala Cynwyd, Pa., a culturally distinct society, each of whose members owns their own Cuisinart and can hum at least one tune by Noel Coward with a mouthful of soda crackers.)

So strong is the correlation that the most sought-after dinner guests in Bala Cynwyd are almost always those occupying the loftiest rungs of the Merion Lawn and Cricket Club tennis ladder, while those on the "B" Team at the YMCA are invariably last-minute substitutes, relegated to folding chairs on the veranda, out near the maiden aunts and potted plants. Indeed, when the most lionized wit of Bala Cynwyd developed tennis elbow, the flood of invitations delivered to his home diminished to a sporadic trickle of tickets to Kiwanis Club potluck suppers, his wife of nineteen years suddenly divorced him, and his Mercedes was found one morning covered with hex signs and Pennsylvania Dutch graffiti.

The anthropologists found that many of the couples most esteemed as scintillating conversationalists were actually dullards with

Tennis, Anyone?

low I.Q.s, small frontal lobes and an educational history as fleeting as a tennis prodigy's. Although constantly on the verge of utter confusion and speechlessness whenever the conversation ranged beyond the vagaries of the local real estate market, these experienced guests were able not only to keep conversation after conversation alive but eventually to become the mainstays of their gourmet clubs simply by staying cautiously on the baseline of non-committal remarks and throwing up dull, conversational lobs at the first hint of trouble. Notes taken furtively by the anthropologists on slightly risqué cocktail napkins showed, for example, that when asked for an opinion about presidential candidates, a conversational lobber replied, "What do you think?;" when informed of some subtle property of black holes, she said, "How cute!;" and when invited to comment on a pet theory of economics by the person on her left, she scrunched up her nose in the manner of Tracy Austin and began an animated conversation about mortgage rates with the person on her right.

A common fault observed by the anthropologists was the failure to protect the conversational alley. One such example was transcribed by several of the anthropologists on their lobster bibs. A young couple were asked how many children they had. The husband answered "Four" at exactly the moment the wife said "Two." Unfortunately, the rest of this episode, which led to one of the juiciest divorces in the annals of Bucks County, Pa., has been lost to social science, having been rendered indecipherable by a blob of seafood sauce.

Jim Kobak

The correlation between tennis ranking and social standing, though dimly perceived by most participants, was clearly drawn in the eleven-hour monologue of Henrietta Budge-Laver-Tilden, the octogenarian Grande Dame of Bala Cynwyd society and holder of sixty-seven mixed doubles titles, to which the anthropologists were treated over daiquiris at B-L-T, the Budge-Laver-Tilden ancestral estate. None of the anthropologists has any recollection of this session, but the matriarch's imperious, pear-shaped tones could clearly be heard for miles, and portions of the conversation have been preserved on neighbors' tape recorders.

Approximately ten hours and fifty-nine minutes of the monologue bear a strong resemblance to complete gibberish, representing as they do a recitation of a Main Line railroad schedule memorized by Ms. Budge-Laver-Tilden as a teenager in order to while away the hours spent away from the tennis court. The crux of the monologue occurs in a brief pause between the 8:48 from North Philadelphia and the 8:46 from Chestnut Hill. In that momentary hiatus Ms. Budge-Laver-Tilden announced with breathtaking clarity the simple precepts that have so successfully guided her conduct:

>Always pass the pepper with the salt.

>Never throw your salad fork or your tennis racquet at the Queen of England.

>Dance the night away with the tennis pro but always go home with the one who brought you,

> especially if the one who brought you is
> wealthy and puts you in his will.

The anthropologists reportedly found the study "immensely rewarding," perhaps because they received hundreds of free meals and collectively ran off with one heiress, four sets of silverware, and innumerable coasters and ashtrays. Whether their results can be replicated outside Pennsylvania (and particularly in a jurisdiction that does not recognize extradition to that state), who knows? Just remember, if some anthropologists appear at your doorstep, the only sure way to get rid of them is to offer them some goose liver pate.

Jim Kobak

Professional Tennis and You

Watching professional tennis matches requires adjustment of the skills and techniques used to play tennis. This is because the tennis played at events such as the U.S. Open bears no relationship to the activity that you know as tennis.

First, tennis pros are athletes. Tennis pros hit tennis balls behind their backs; they hit tennis balls with their eyes closed; they hit tennis balls while listening to their Walkmen and iPods, chatting with their accountants, and getting telephone numbers from tawny-haired tennis groupies wandering by at courtside. Hours of practice have given tennis pros the legs of ballet dancers, the hearts of marathon runners, and the arms of farmers and plowmen. Spectators such as you lack this essential equipment, having instead the legs of accountants, the hearts of dentists, and arms that hold plates at buffets.

Second, tennis players never have to play with balls like those you use. Scarcely have a few games been played and the first few pieces of fuzz wafted off into the air over Paris, Wimbledon, or Flushing Meadows than the old balls are discarded and replaced by new ones still warm from the tennis ball factory. Not for the pros the bald, discolored things that you know as tennis balls: those dense globules of matter found under sofas trailing clouds of debris; or those mildewed pellets that leave wet spots on the court, are covered with molds never yet seen in a Petrie dish, and have been sucked, bitten, and orally abused by babies, unidentified forest creatures and lawn mowers. Tennis as you know it is not new balls after nine and eleven games, as it is for the tennis pros. More likely, it is new balls after nine or eleven weeks—if you have a birthday or anniversary coming up or it is around Christmas time.

Finally, tennis players do not find tennis as tiring as you do because it does not take them as long to get to the ball. They can cover the sides of the court with a *grand jeté* or two and easily span the chasm between baseline and net in five or six steps. To cover the same ground, you must work much harder. Think of the number of steps you take to get from the net to the baseline, should someone risk expulsion from the country club by throwing up a deep lob: fifteen, perhaps? twenty? thirty or more if there are interesting plants along the way?

One way to come to terms with the difference between professional tennis and what it is that you do on a tennis court is to compare the beginning of a professional match with the start of one or your own sessions on the court. At the start of the professional match the players appear in garments emblazoned with endorsements. Each carries at least eight or ten rackets—more than you can lift. They rally for a few minutes; feeding each other volleys and overheads. Then the umpire introduces them, reciting a list of tournament results in the last six months that is three times as long as your curriculum vitae and appears to mention every place listed in the Official Airline Guide.

Visualize now the *mise-en-scène* when you prepare to play tennis. Your tennis garb is a little frayed about the seams, more than a little tight about the waist; the footwear is two parts shoe-glue for every part shoe. It has obviously been an ordeal simply dressing for the match. No endorsements adorn your sleeves. In fact, the nether parts of the faded alligator on your tennis whites became unstitched so long ago that the alligator has curled itself up into the shape of a sleeping armadillo.

Your warm up sessions are mostly spent chasing balls that have rolled to neighboring courts and sailed over distant fences. There is, needless to say, no umpire.

If there were an umpire, the introduction would proceed roughly as follows:

"To the chair's right is Mr. Oblomov, who is currently ranked fifth in his own household. That, however, was before his recent tennis lesson.

Mr. Oblomov's opponent is Nicholas Bartleby. The owner of a brand new Fila warm up suit, Mr. Bartleby recently came close to accomplishing his personal Grand Slam—that is, hitting four backhands in a row against a backboard.

The players have elected to play with Mr. Oblomov's tennis balls as they are "almost like new," having only been used three times and chewed briefly by Mr. Oblomov's golden retriever. Rather than changing balls at nine and eleven games, balls will be changed only

Tennis, Anyone?

when the initial ones have been struck to locations that the players deem too far away to bother with retrieval.

In the event the score reaches six all, the players will not play a tiebreaker inasmuch as they are all pretty fuzzy on what the rules of a tiebreaker are, and Mr. Bartleby has to leave by 4:45 to get to the laundry before it closes. In any event, it is unlikely that the players would have the energy to continue if they have played as many as twelve games!

There is an important corollary to the differences between the game of tennis as played at the lofty professional level and the game of tennis as played by you: it is much more difficult for you to watch a tennis match than it is for the players to play in it. This is where the adjustments come in. Plan and prepare accordingly, and never stray far from beer, sangria, or other suitable refreshment.

Consider a typical five-set match several years ago at the U.S. Open between Heinz Günthardt and Henri LeConte. After the six grueling hours were over, Günthardt went off, not to check in to intensive care, but to play tennis doubles with Martina Navratilova, Balas Taroczy, or anyone else having a long, unpronounceable name. LeConte, the valiant loser, sat around looking as dejected as Edith Piaf for about a minute and a half, then remembered that he had a beautiful wife, waved to the crowd and went off to disco the night away.

The audience, however, had had to sit in a cramped, unnatural position for hours, virtually deprived of speech, intermittently forced to clap their hands, and insidiously exposed to a fierce sun for which their previous sojourns in movie theaters and delis had left them grievously unprepared. The players had been given one and one half-minute rests between games. The audience, however, had been given no rests, no towels, and scarcely even a sporting opportunity to visit the rest room. While Günthardt volleyed and LeConte danced, the audience recuperated for hours after the match, gulping down nachos and jalapeno cheese for extra energy.

A final corollary to the ease with which professional tennis players play tennis may by now have occurred to you: they should really pay you for watching rather than vice versa. As a matter of logic, this is quite sound. Unfortunately, the players' union and their accountants and tawny-haired tennis groupies long ago adopted rules which prevent it.

Tennis, Anyone?

A Poetic Coda to Professional Tennis and You: The Torments of the Tournaments

The Warm Up

From forth to back
The ball, well smacked,
So smoothly goes
When struck just so.

The Play

Let play commence
And all grows tense
And now some lout
Keeps shouting, "Out!"

Do ears deceive?
Can one conceive
That I hit wrong
And much too long?

Too soon my nerves
Undo my serves
And fill with dread
Each overhead.

Too soon abort
My lobs hit short
While all my gets
End in the net.

Taught skills recede
As points proceed
And sets, though brief,
Are filled with grief.

The Denouement

Words cruel and terse
Though well-rehearsed
Must end this verse
And match accursed
By gods above.
I've lost six love.

Tennis, Anyone?

Using Artificial Intelligence to Improve Your Tennis

An interesting new way to try to sharpen up your game is to use artificial intelligence. But here is a tip for you: It is generally more productive to play against artificial intelligence as an opponent than with artificial intelligence as a partner. This is because, while AI employs all manner of complicated vectors and sophisticated formulae to determine where a ball will land, it is unable to move on its own to get that to place and covers even less of the court than you do. It is also unable to pick up any of the tennis balls that accumulate on your side of the court .

Artificial intelligence likes to be called Art, Artie, or sometimes, Artemnesia, but even with these attempts at humanizing and ingratiating itself AI remains relatively useless as a partner—and, like many human partners, prone to barking out instructions and offering critiques. Whether calling itself Art or using some other alias, AI uses much the same repertoire of clichés and insults as your partners, but adapts them to your own idiosyncratic fears and phobias which it finds on the internet. One redeeming feature of AI is that you can program it to speak in foreign languages so you do not have to understand what it is saying, like the foreign films that have won awards at festivals that you are forced to watch with your spouse or significant other. You can also say, "Shut up, Art," or, "Zip it,

Artemnisia," and put him, her, or it on mute. This you cannot do with a human partner unless you have a gun.

To get started, put a laptop loaded with Chat Box or some variant on the other side of the net and hit a tennis ball in its general direction. You will see that Artemnesia, for all her fancy vocabulary, can't move an inch and doesn't have a racquet or any other implement with which to hit the ball. There is thus a good chance that you will be able to win many points—provided only that you yourself can hit a ball over the net and have it land somewhere within all those lines on the other side of the court. But beware that should you hit a ball close to a line, AI will never give you the benefit of the doubt as human opponents may do—well, a few opponents once in a while anyway—but will use precise GPS data to determine conclusively that your ball was out. While you may consider these calls unsportsmanlike, they will be supported by NASA, the CIA, and the Public Broadcasting System and may be appealed only to the World Court in the Hague, generally a cumbersome process even if you happen to be playing in Belgium (which is where AI tells me the Hague is located and Artemnesia thinks she was born).

While it initially seems gratifying to win points without expenditure of much effort against a disembodied mental construct that exists only on a metaphysical plane, it eventually becomes rather boring, like most encounters with metaphysics. So to liven things up a little, try to give Art some mobility. Hook the laptop up to a Roomba, and Artie will figure out how to program the Roomba to move where AI calculated the ball will land. AI, now in the guise of Artemnesia, tells me that it is fun to be riding around on the top of a Roomba: what she divines it might be like for a human to tool around Belgium on a motorcycle. Another advantage of using the Roomba is that one never has to sweep the court after play.

Art, having returned to replace Artie and Artemnesia while they are preoccupied with Belgium, now notes that combining AI with the Roomba, while a probably patentable technological advance, is still an incomplete solution because he and the Roomba have no way to hit the ball once they have reached it. Only very infrequently can Art maneuver the Roomba so that a ball will strike it in such a way that it rebounds over a tennis net.

A few hours of play will confirm that Art has indeed identified a serious design flaw. One solution is to attach the now superfluous broom lying uselessly on the side of the court to the Roomba. This would give Art a potential means for hitting the ball. Artie, having returned from a museum crawl in Belgium, can't resist chiming in and calls the resulting assemblage ungainly, primitive, and contrived, comparing it to many examples of modern sculpture. But it does mean that at least a few balls made it to the other side of the court, albeit often covered with straw.

Of course AI has a tendency to hallucinate from time to time, and there could be occasions when it may confuse the Roomba with the rhumba, leading to moves seldom observed on a tennis court. But needless to say, AI is not the only one who hallucinates from time to time; by asking Art and Artie to adopt their Artemnesia persona, and then you yourself putting on a tux, it is possible to envision the two of you cutting quite a rug at the country club dance.

Alas, one unfortunate consequence of having AI as a tennis opponent is that, unlike most of my human acquaintances, when it is not hallucinating, AI is always thinking. So it hasn't taken Art long to develop a method for connecting not just a broom to the Roomba but a military-grade drone. This technology makes for a formidable opponent indeed. Balls now rain down on one's side of the court from improbable angles, at warp speed, and with consummate power, shredding expensive tennis gear, obliterating lines, and leaving craters in the service box. The drone also makes a raucous buzzing noise even more annoying than the ping of pickle ball rackets, leading to complaints from players on adjacent courts, onlookers, and of course the residents of Scarsdale. The existence of these complainants is of little concern to Art, whose drones can obliterate them, along with any lurking terrorists.

An awkward aspect of playing with AI is how to handle the obligatory handshake at the end of the session on the court. Art has been programmed to regurgitate the standard post-match platitudes: Nice game." "We should do it again." "How long did you say you have been playing?" "You have an interesting way of playing for someone who must never have had any lessons." But none of AI's human avatars, not even Artie or Artemnesia, actually has a hand or, for that matter, any body part to shake. Shaking hands with a broom is uncomfortable at best and leaves lint and who knows what else on your fingers. On the other hand, the alternative of high-fiving a drone is ill-advised and likely to lead to grievous injury and even loss of limb. A good way to handle this inevitable inconvenience is to bow or curtsey as if parting from royalty while surreptitiously sidling toward the laptop to turn it off and put up for sale on eBay. Just remember to move quickly before the drone gets you.

Jim Kobak

Tennis Meets STEM: What Developments Like the Space Telescope Mean for Racquet Sports

Many racket sport enthusiasts fail to appreciate science or the role that something like the powerful Webb space telescope may come to play in the future of tennis and related sports. The non-golfing, non-bicycling faction of the astrophysics community who are tennis and paddle tennis afficionados has already divined that having a huge telescope will greatly enhance the accuracy of line calls, determining whether even the smallest particle of fuzz from a ball does or does not impinge on a strip of tape or painted surface, even one that a player has tried scuffing out with his feet while calling a ball out. At the amateur level, the giant telescope could be useful for spotting vacant outdoor tennis courts and indoor squash courts. At the professional level, it will aid in ultra-clear detection and magnification of the trademarks and corporate logos on players' clothing.

But of course most scientists are training this massive telescope not on the grass at Wimbledon but into the farthest reaches of outer space. Discoveries of great interest even to the most casual of pickle ball players are being made nearly every day. For example, the telescope can peer into the primordial origins of space and time to gain insight into the uncertainty principle that underlies our understanding of the movement of matter. This in turn could lead to insights into the tennis play of you and your tennis partner which, though only sporadically involving much movement of matter, is rife with uncertainty.

Most exciting of all is the search for new universes and the possibility of so-called exo-planets. That's right: planets sprinkled around this or other universes that are similar to earth but are X-rated in real life, not only on the internet. (Astrophysicists use terms like *multiverse* and *exo-planet* rather than *porn sites* and *X-rated* to remain being eligible for grant money and avoid being thought of as peeping toms.)

Think of the possibilities of discovering planets with infinite variations of tennis, racquet ball, handball, and perhaps even volleyball and Newcomb, to say nothing of infinite numbers of tennis tournaments, advertising and sponsorship opportunities, and country club initiation fees. Already one particularly sharp-eyed space telescope technician has tentatively identified an extraterrestrial object that appears to consist of cages housing lined surfaces; these appear to some experts to represent either penal colonies or places where racquet sports are played, or perhaps both. A post doc who has to moonlight as a tennis pro to make ends meet speculates that these facilities may constitute a sort of ur-form of racquet sport from which all the elements of tennis, pickle ball, squash, paddle tennis, badminton, ping pong and possibly even lacrosse and the ritual Aztec ball game are derived. This may also ultimately explain the odd scoring systems, rules, and protocols embedded in these surviving progeny of this ancestral, Platonic form of time-wasting recreation.

Since this discovery involved an exo- or X-rated planet, some at NASA and on the space craft Mir theorize (or perhaps more accurately, fantasize) that players inside the cages participated in the nude. Points may have been awarded for striking particular parts of other players' anatomies, with sponsors' logos tattooed on carefully selected body parts. None, however, are intrepid enough to hazard even a guess about what this might have entailed for the primitive version of what we now call pickle ball.

To some, the appearance of these cages with markings evocative of racquet sports play is suggestive of the presence of intelligent life forms. Others agree that evidence of possible racquet sport activity does suggest the existence of life but question whether life that engages in this activity can be considered intelligent.

Tennis, Anyone?

The Culinary Aspects of Tennis and Other Racquet Sports

If you have read this far in the book you are probably getting hungry. And tennis and other racquet sports afford all sorts of opportunities for dinner parties, luncheons, banquets, and other festive gatherings. Jai alai itself means "merry festival" and if the name were not trademarked and subject to the harsh infringement penalties of Basque intellectual property law, it could be applied to any of the related sports mentioned in this book. Serving racquet-themed foods always adds zest and opportunities for repartee that will make any social function at least as merry as a jai alai tournament conducted by Mexican gambling and narcotics cartels.

For example, you can invite your pickle ball group, the membership of your tennis club, or all the residents of Scarsdale, New York, and Wimbledon, England, to a banquet where you serve only game, like venison, moose, various waterfowl, and any stray foxes you may encounter still prowling around Scarsdale. You can call this a tennis or pickle ball or some other Game Night and not only serve game but also have everyone play a game like Trivial Pursuit with the only categories being racquet sports and the mating habits of wildlife. Or try a more esoteric game like chess, with specially designed pieces people could take home in their goody bags: a Roger Federer statuette as king, Serena Williams as queen, miniature ball boys and boy girls as pawns, bishops holding tennis rackets rather than croziers, and Billy Jean King figurines as the white knights and Bobby Riggs figurines as the opposing ones. (For a less esoteric crowd, substitute the game Sorry, since the frequent repetition of that word and the general lack of skill required in the game will resonate with many of your guests' tennis court experiences.)

No matter what the diversion chosen, after a few glasses of schnapps a dinner of game dishes always generates conversation and that staple of social life, complaints and catty remarks. There will be all manner of references to turkeys, ball hogs, and, after a few more glasses of schnapps, dinosaurs and old fossils and (for badminton) bird brains. It has probably occurred to you already that squash would be an obvious side dish for such a dinner. And because there are so many varieties of squash, it is also quite feasible to hold an all-squash gala for vegan and vegetarian players .

The spaghetti racquet never really took off as a piece of tennis equipment, but that doesn't mean its design can't make for some great canapés. It does take practice and a certain amount of innate dexterity to mold strands of spaghetti into the shape of a miniature tennis racket, to say nothing of topping them off with a lilliputian, carefully balanced game- or squash-based ball. So it is best to have extra napkins available, especially for the cocktail hour. Some hosts and hostesses have been known to substitute linguini for the spaghetti and to hand guests string cheese so they can string their own racquets. This approach works best

Tennis, Anyone?

if your guest list includes tennis pros and sporting goods store owners with very small hands.

A racquet sport-themed event may be held almost anywhere, but an elegant touch can be added by doing it at one's home. For the many readers with their own indoor squash and tennis courts, this can be easily done. The household staff need merely be reminded that tonight's dinner will not be served in either the Grand Pavilion or the Great Ball Room and that they are going to need to touch up the Giotto frescoes on the ceiling of the squash court and bring the Caravaggios down from the attic to hang on its walls. Those recently down on their luck and temporarily lacking their own extensive indoor sports facilities can always make do by setting up an old ping pong table, dents and all, and Windexing it vigorously to remove the grime and mold that have adhered to it during the years it has been stored away in the dark and dingy basement. (Hint: If the grime and mold can't be removed, hang the table on the wall and call it a Pollock or Chaim Soutine.) No matter what type of table or court is used, it is customary for those continuing with their game while the food is being consumed to play a let—technically called a food service fault—when the ball hits a guest, servant or eating utensil or lands in the spaghetti.

This is not to suggest that all tennis-themed meals need be elegant soirées. Far from it. You can have enjoyable informal brunches or pleasant visits to food trucks with your tennis partners or opponents. Think bagels, if you have just beaten someone six-love. Or poached eggs. These can form the basis not only for the eggs benedict but heart-to-heart conversations about feelings triggered by fellow diners' on court behavior patterns.

There are almost as many kinds of pickles as there are varieties of squash, so arranging meals for pickle ball players is, as it were, duck soup (though putting pickles in the duck soup is not recommended). There are even more pickle ball players than there are varieties of either squash or pickles, and their numbers are growing exponentially so be sure to order lots of pickles and rent a large tent. You can also pickle just about anything and serve it to guests, especially guests to whom you lose frequently. In fact, you should be aware of the risk of pickling yourself through careless or profligate intake of the cooking sherry in the pantry during meal prep—though I do find that sometimes moderate intake of cooking sherry can ease the strain of making conversation with former tennis partners and spouses and their lawyers and security details.

To be a good neighbor to those unable or unwilling to attend an event in person, drop off something from time to time at their front porch, apartment door, or the guardhouse by the moat surrounding their castle. You can call it a service box lunch, something likely to bring a smile to the lips of even the most curmudgeonly recluse or jaded Buckingham Palace guard. Slice a roll in half, put some salami on it and call it an Italian Open sub. Or take the leftovers from the event you went to great toil and trouble to hold, dump them all in a bag, liberally apply pickle brine, shake it all up, and write a note on the bag letting the person who would not deign to attend or even to RSVP that this is their just desert—and that you have eaten what would have been their actual dessert.

A tennis-themed meal can also become a costume party. Indeed, you might even be able to organize a pot luck or BYOC (bring your own chef) party, shifting much of the anxiety about event preparation from your already fatigued shoulders to those of the guests. You can then relax and even have time to practice your tennis while they are preoccupied in planning, worrying, texting one another, shopping, consulting cookbooks and fashion designers, and in some rare cases even sewing and embroidering.

There is much to be said about a racquet-themed costume party. It is one thing to see an hors d'oeuvre in the shape of a spaghetti racquet or pickle, but quite another to see a five foot eleven inch tall human spaghetti racquet cavorting on the dance floor with a five foot one inch lady pickle. And the same can be said for the lithe, lightly feathered wild turkey with a Lester Lanin hat on her head doing the Watutsi with a tall, black-robed bishop carrying a paddle.

And now that you have come up with all these ideas for a racquet-themed event, it is time for you, as the creative idea person, to form the committee and turn everything over to them to organize and pay for. This might or might not lead to an actual party full of people talking incessantly about tennis. It might or might not lead to the breakup of your tennis partnership. And whether these results might be good or bad, who can say?

Tennis, Anyone?

The Rules Quiz

You may have gotten this far in the book, but how well do you really know the rules, customs, and codes of decorum governing tennis and other racquet sports? Take the following short quiz to find out.

1. Being a player who plays tennis and serves left-handed is
   A. No fun for anyone else
   B. Cheating
   C. Grounds for disqualification not only from future matches but any office of the United States.

2. Being a good athlete who plays tennis is
   A. Something that your tennis group has no rule about because it so seldom comes up
   B. By definition, someone who should take up squash
   C. Unfathomable to most of us.

3. Being a good athlete who plays tennis and serves left-handed is
   A. An outrage
   B. A crime against the rest of humanity
   C. Grounds for impeachment as well as disqualification, loss of parking privileges and having your car towed to the pound.

4. Which of the following do the rules of most racquet sports forbid throwing on the court:
   A. The racquet
   B. A knife, spear or javelin
   C. A tantrum
   D. If betting is involved, the outcome of a match.

5. Which of the following rules or principles of the legal system also apply to tennis and other racquet sports?
   A. The Rule of Perpetuity, if the same family has reserved a court for the lifetimes of all family members in being plus ninety-nine years
   B. The rule in Shelly's case, if you or your partner is named Shelly
   C. The exclusionary rule, in the case of players who poach, don't pay their dues or are over-confident, athletic and left-handed

6. When you hit an opponent, partner, ball girl or mere passerby with an errant shot but the ball nevertheless caroms into the court, you should
   A. Play a let
   B. Say nothing until you have called your lawyer
   C. Carry on as if nothing untoward has happened
   D. Run for your life

7. Which of the following is never tolerated on the tennis court?
   A. Train whistles
   B. Wolf whistles
   C. Mechanical whistles, kazoos, harmonicas or accordion-like instruments of any kind

8. On the other hand, what is known as "whistle blowing" is allowed, and even encouraged, in which of the following circumstances?
   A. When a player consistently calls "out" opponents' shots that have landed clearly on or within the lines
   B. When an opponent who claims to be right-handed unleashes a powerful, devilishly spinning lefthanded serve
   C. When someone has stolen your racquet, paddle or online identity

Tennis, Anyone?

    D. When your boss is the person who stole your racquet and has been making unwanted sexual advances in the workplace, cooking the corporate books, and happens to be a certain former president of the United States

9. A carom shot may be played
   A. In some forms of paddle tennis
   B. In squash, if you know how or get lucky once in a while
   C. In Nok-Hockey but not pickle ball, despite their other similarities
   D. In badminton, if playing indoors in a building with low ceilings or when playing outdoors on an untended court with many trees

10. The Bob Dylan song "Blowing in the Wind" was written
    A. To call attention to racial and social injustice and as a paean to radical change
    B. To explain why so many of his shots went awry when Bob Dylan played tennis with the members of the Band before they became the Band
    C. Because Dylan wanted to know whether the answer to question number 7 above did or did or did not permit him to play his harmonica on the tennis court

Jim Kobak

Another Tennis Villanelle

Wow, all these tests are a lot of work, so it's time for another break with another poem. To further relieve stress, read it aloud to your yogi or spiritual advisor in your favorite meditation pose or to yourself while dozing off with a beer on the couch.

Tennis Villanelle 2

With such stray steps and slow we move about
Hard court or clay, as stiff as mannequins,
As every ball we hit too late goes out.

Not well do forays to the net work out:
In each other's way and not in unison,
With such stray steps and slow we move about.

"Sorry" and "Oy vey" all day we shout.
We pray that wayward forehands might fall in
As every ball we hit too late goes out.

Assurance frays; each new point breeds new doubt;
Technique gives way as soon as game begins;
With such stray steps and slow we move about.

Tennis, Anyone?

Ball toss agley; faults called on service mount;
Bad habits same as they have always been
As every ball we hit too late goes out.

The score today? Love-six or thereabouts.
"Well played," opponents lie with ruthless grins.
With such stray steps and slow we move about
As every ball we hit too late goes out.

Jim Kobak

Tennis and Theology

Is there tennis after death? This question has vexed theologians, philosophers, mystics, and manufacturers of tennis paraphernalia for centuries. Some people, looking no farther than their own tennis partner, say "yes" unequivocally. They note that that person seldom moves or speaks and looks, for all practical purposes, like an inert mass on a tennis court. He or she is often referred to metaphorically as so much dead weight, and in fact, even if you were a doctor it would be difficult to determine whether your partner were alive or dead. If they are dead but still considered an active member of your tennis group, there must, as a matter of logic, be tennis after death, QED, and, as afterlives go, it even appears to be a relatively benign, non-stressful and non-arduous one. These people also ask what they would possibly do if there were no tennis in the afterlife. Would they spend eternity in complete oblivion, or what amounts to the same thing, thinking only about golf and watching replays of old PGA events spooling forever on an endless celestial TV monitor occupying all of time and space?

Others believe this reasoning is far too simplistic. They postulate that tennis, in order to retain its quiddity and identity as tennis, must retain its essential character as torture and a source of frustration, even if it were to be played by incorporeal beings after death. These thinkers believe that no deity could be so cruel as to inflict tennis and other racquet sports on our earthly existence and then perpetuate that misery after death. They posit that Christ's comment that his father's house had many mansions must mean that there is more than just a golf channel capable of filling an eternal void. There could, they think, be movies with subtitles and Simpson episodes. There could be HD operas, Beatles songs, and Linda Ronstadt in concert, all streaming in celestial harmony. The Beatles might even be reunited if there is a heaven. There might be popcorn as well as ambrosia.

Logical positivists and other naysayers scoff at all this talk of popcorn in paradise as so much poppycock. They point out that this reasoning presupposes a deity with at least the benevolence of a veterinarian willing to put a suffering, incurable pet out of inescapable misery. But how could such a being have seen fit to inflict tennis on the world in the first place, with its Sisyphean courts that must be incessantly rolled, watered, swept and re-lined only to be replaced by pickle ball courts? And why do we suppose that an omniscient deity would go to veterinary school?

Some other less philosophically inclined agnostics observe that tennis players pray frequently that their shots will go in, that they won't double fault on set point, that they won't be late for their tennis game, and that their tennis clothes from last season will still fit, etc., Yet observation teaches that these prayers are almost never answered.

Many theologians believe that mankind was doomed from the moment Eve first plucked an apple and noticed that it was roundish in shape and if painted yellow or white might serve as a tennis ball. At about the same time, it dawned on Adam, while trying to cover his private parts, that putting a graphite frame on the leaf he was using for that purpose would allow him to use it as a racket if he could only find a pair of pants somewhere. We have paid the price for that forbidden knowledge ever since, and not even the suffering of Rafael Nadal, the complaints of John McEnroe, or the intervention of the Williams sisters can redeem us. A few saintly role models like Billy Jean King, Chris Evert, and Martina Navratilova or Roger Federer may receive halos and the stigmata; for the rest of us, it is sunburn and tennis elbow. Meanwhile, Satan gloats in the wings as the racquet sports we invented with his connivance beget every sin from avarice and envy through vainglory and wrath. And thus are we doomed to poach, foot fault, and shuffle our way through life and into eternity with the sun forever in our eyes and a chip always on our shoulders.

This leads us to the knotty issue of predestination, the subject of convocations, councils, and synods more tempestuous than the most heated Davis Cup match. Religious leaders from Augustine and Aquinas to John Calvin have pondered the balance between the perfect knowledge of past and future possessed by an all-knowing God and whether that leaves any room for free will for the rest of us. More recently, some biologists have been trying to prove that our genes predetermine our every action so we not only have no free will but, like a certain former president, no culpability for any of our actions.

If predestination exists, either in theology or biology or both, it has profound implications for tennis, for racquet sports in general, and for sports betting, both during our earthly existence and beyond. Do we choose which racquet sport to take up or are we unconsciously and irresistibly compelled to take up pickle ball, tennis, handball, or badminton? Would we possibly take up any of these things if we acted consciously and exercised free will? Are the inhabitants of earth condemned to categories such as golfer, tennis player, or bowler—or for the elect few, couch potato-- from the moment of their birth; from the moment of their creation, icky as that is to contemplate; or from the moment of the Big Bang? Was Taylor Swift always destined to be Taylor Swift while you were always destined to be number 13 on a twelve-runged tennis ladder?

Of course, predestination could afford comforting explanations for many puzzling aspects of your tennis game. For example, it could explain why you have never been able to put away an easy overhead or bend your knees for a low volley. It could be the explanation for the futility of all your tennis lessons. It may explain why you tripped over your hat going back for that lob; why you stumbled over it again rushing to the net; and why you always seem to stumble and fare so badly not only on pickle ball and tennis courts but, even when hatless, in divorce and criminal courts. Perhaps no amount of due diligence on the tennis court or in other aspects of your life could have prevented your spouse from having such a splendid time in Nice without you—or you from languishing all that time in solitary confinement in the

Eastern State Penitentiary.

But at the end of the day, will you be truly satisfied that every incident in your life has been predetermined? Couldn't you have decided to buy that sailboat after all and died a watery death rather than a hot and dusty one on a red clay tennis court? Pelages thought "yes" (though he never, as far as anyone knows, ever bought a sail boat), but he was denounced as a heretic by St. Augustine, excommunicated, and led an impoverished, abstemious life with a small band of followers confined to a squash court with no ball or racquet. On the other hand, Augustine himself later on, and then even Thomas Aquinas, began hedging their bets and saying well, maybe, just maybe, in some circumstances and to some extent there could be a narrow space, like the alleys on a tennis court, for people to make some choices.

But it will take many pages of medieval Latin text and a lot of head scratching to try to understand all of this. It will be almost as hard as trying to decipher the examples and advice of a tennis instructor. So you may as well treat it all like a tennis lesson—best either foregone or forgotten completely—and play on, as blissfully oblivious as ever to the cause, constancy, and cumulative effect of your blunders.

Tennis, Anyone?

Looking Ahead: Some Thoughts About the Future of Racquet Sports

While tennis and racquet sports in general may seem steeped in tradition, as other chapters have demonstrated, these sports have continued to change and adapt over time. From misty, ancient origins court tennis arose as a pursuit for the nobility, like jousting or writing sonnets, but over time has evolved into the sport of the masses we know today, just as jousting evolved into NASCAR and sonnets into tweets. So too, squash and squash courts assumed a new dimension as they left the courtyards of Harrow in order to gain a place in a larger, more adult world.

Adaptation is in fact a hallmark of racquet sports. The world became warmer and wetter as the icebergs and glaciers melted; tennis raised itself onto platforms and became paddle tennis. It moved indoors with the advent of unpredictable storms and adoption of air conditioning and accommodated itself to surfaces other than grass as weather deteriorated, the costs of fertilizer rose, and ticks carrying Lyme disease proliferated. Then it morphed again, into squash and racquet ball. We began to notice that the world was becoming more crowded and our attention spans shorter and along came pickle ball, a condensed form of tennis spreading around the globe on the very courts of its predecessor.

How might tennis and racquet sports develop and grow in the

future? One way might be to incorporate elements that have proved successful in other sports. For example, there are faults and lost points galore in a tennis match but, despite the behaviors so often observed on court, virtually no fouls or penalties. Yet fouls and penalties are a prominent, and often the most discussed, features of many other sports like football, basketball hockey, and even soccer. It does not take much imagination to catalogue designated infractions from other sports that could apply equally to tennis: tripping, high sticking, offsides or encroachment, roughing and unnecessary roughness, and of course delay of game, to name a few.

In hockey, players who commit infractions are confined to a penalty box outside the area of play; in some soccer leagues the same thing is beginning to happen to offending footballers, with players placed in what are called "sin bins." These concepts could easily be added to tennis play at all levels, from grand slam tournaments to your Tuesday tennis group. Think how much provocative discussion could ensue—and how much safer members of your group might feel—if a player could be forcibly restrained from playing against you (or even with you) for a point or two, an entire season, or the rest of their lives, unless pardoned by the governor.

Suitable names for areas of temporary confinement include "fault zone," "the poaching pan" (for some partners who shall be nameless), purgatory or limbo. There could also be penalty shots administered by Dr. Fauci, penalty kicks administered by you, or a system in which players are handed out colored cards, as in professional soccer. These could include not only yellow and red cards but also library cards, forcing one to read tennis books like this one in underground stacks surrounded by procrastinating graduate students unable to complete their dissertations; a MetroCard, forcing one to ride a crowded F train at rush hour dressed in tennis whites; or a meal card, forcing one to stand on line in a high school cafeteria during match point. A card might even read, "Take a ride on the Reading, do not pass Go, do not collect $200" (for players from Pennsylvania). "Corner time" is also a possible alternative to corporal punishment for those misbehaving during paddle tennis games.

Not only are soccer players sometimes allowed a penalty kick, but golf has penalty strokes for hitting a ball out of bounds or into the water. This feature, too, could be added to sports like badminton and tennis to deal with overly energetic players at lakeside resorts. In biathlon, when one misses a target, one must ski a penalty loop. So too in pickle ball might one serving overhand or standing too long in the kitchen be required to play thereafter on skis. (Cautionary note: Guns are involved in biathlon, but their use in racquet sports is not recommended, except in Texas, where they are of course mandatory, especially for doubles matches.)

Lobs are the bane of many a tennis player's existence. Much of that angst could be relieved if tennis simply borrowed the infield fly rule from baseball. In the dimly understood circumstances when this rule is invoked, no one need actually catch a ball that a batter has hit high in the summer sky; the batter is automatically declared "out." If Phil Rizzuto or Derek Jeter could twiddle their thumbs and safely ignore balls hit way above their heads in the middle of a game, why can't you?

Perhaps racquet sports in the future will go even farther than adopting rules from other sports. They may repurpose equipment, as they did with the whiffle ball in the case of pickle ball. Consider, for example, the effect that a hockey puck—or, for that matter, a hockey stick or a scarily decorated hockey goalie's mask—might have on a previously friendly paddle tennis game. Or how transformative it could be to replace birdies with lacrosse balls and skinny little rackets with defensemen's lacrosse sticks in pick up family badminton games on the Fourth of July. And as food for further thought, there are always bocce balls and croquet mallets.

What someone did with an old whiffle ball revolutionized tennis. An aging hippie found an old frisbee and now we have frisbee golf. There is probably lots of old stuff in your basement or garage: nerf balls, scuba gear, deflated basketballs, the bean bag things you pick up and throw in cornhole. Look around. Be creative. Stop reading (after having paid for the book, of course). Get up from your chair and start clearing out that musty basement. It could be the key to your future and the future of generations of racquet sport enthusiasts yet unborn. And

Tennis, Anyone?

if not, you might pick up a few dollars from the yard sale—if you are lucky, almost enough to pay for a new can of tennis balls.

Jim Kobak

An Ode to My Tennis Partners

It seemed fitting to end this work with either a dedicatory or valedictory tribute to those with whom I have shared so many hours on so many courts. so here goes:

If we had all of time and space
My dear, you'd never hit an ace.
A redwood tree could grow and rot
Before you hit a passing shot.

The Andes will be grains of sand
Before you move from where you stand.
The Rockies will be low and flat
Before you hit a service back.

By the time you've reached a tennis ball
A Greece could form, a Rome cold fall.
Whole nations could emerge from blobs
At the rate at which you track down lobs.

Tennis, Anyone?

As slow the bending of your knees,
As histories by Thucydides.
And when you move from place to place
It is at Edward Gibbons' pace.

Erasmus, with his love of folly,
Would be enamored of your volley.
Moliere would laugh and turn handstands
Should he encounter your backhand.

All comedy seems flat and dead
To one who's seen your overhead.
And Feydeau seems solemn, Pope's wit gray,
To one exposed to your net play.

GLOSSARY

A

Ace. A word with a variable meaning, including the following: an unreturnable serve; a star tennis player; and a type of bandage useful as *après* tennis wear. Ace also refers to a card that is good to have when playing black jack, a game more suitable to your level of physical activity than tennis. Playing blackjack will also allow you to lose money without the fuss of joining tennis leagues and country clubs.

Ad In. The bills for the tennis pro, pro shop, and country club assessment have all arrived.

Ad Out. Unfortunately, the money to pay the bills has not.

Australian Open. The bar in the health and tennis club is open long after the courts close, and it has Foster's on tap.

Australian Twist. (a) The Foster's is served with a slice of lemon in it; (b) songs sung to Chubby Checker music by aging white men at tennis players' weddings.

B

Backboard. A large, rectangular object used in tennis practice to take out aggressions and perfect racquet swings. Very satisfying when hit. Can also be used to hit tennis balls against.

Backhand. (a) The only type of compliment ever heard on a tennis court; (b) the stroke used to write post-dated checks to the tennis pro, tennis club, and chiropractor.

Ball Girl. A young woman who fetches tennis balls until she grows old and rich enough to become a debutante.

Ball Gown. Dress worn by a ball girl upon becoming a debutante.

Ball Toss. A way to practice making a salad with a tennis ball rather than tiny pieces of faux corn and balsamic vinegar to avoid making a mess.

Baseline. A good place behind which to stand on the tennis court because it is as far as possible from other players and the tennis ball.

Baseline Lob. A defensive strategy based on the theory of the Maginot Line and just as effective.

Bounce. (a) What a tennis ball does many times before you reach it; (b) what your stomach does many times while you are running to try to reach the ball.

C

Canadian Doubles. A form of international competition in which, because based on the former value of Canadian currency at the time the game developed, it takes two Canadians to play one citizen of any other country.

Catgut. What's left of your cat after your doubles partner gets through with it.

Carpe diem. A Latin term for finding something new to complain about every day that one plays tennis.

Caravaggio. Renaissance painter and tennis enthusiast who fled Rome after killing one Ranuccio Tomassi in a brawl over a disputed tennis score. Set a standard for painting and questioning umpires that even John McEnroe could not match. Caravaggio had previously run afoul of the law by hurling a plate of artichokes in the face of a waiter, setting a standard for restaurant reviews that even Calvin Trilling and the Zagat guide cannot match.

Centre Court. A court in Wimbledon on which the net casts no shadow whatsoever during the summer solstice and which thus forms the fulcrum of the tennis universe. All lesser tennis courts radiate outward from Centre Court through a complex set of epicycles worked out by Ptolemy while playing ptennis with Roscoe pTanner in honor of the Egyptian god Ptah during the pTenth Dynasty. Eventually these epicycles reach the outermost bounds of the tennis firmament and the parched, pitted, patchwork piece of asphalt on which you play. This court is referred to as the Criminal Court, the Divorce Court or the

Tennis, Anyone?

Kangaroo Court, depending on the identity of your opponent.

Changeover. The act of changing ends of the tennis court every two games so that one may be blinded by sun half the afternoon and buffeted by gale force winds the other half.

Country Club Pro. The over-dressed, heavily perfumed woman at the end of the bar.

Court, Margaret Smith. Though often forgotten today, arguably the best woman tennis player ever. Certainly the shrewdest, having married a man named Court to assure herself a stream of royalties from other players after her own playing days were over.

Crosscourt. The Zen-like, purely hypothetical act of hitting a ball on the diagonal even though the ball is a sphere.

Crosscourt shot. A shot executed by an angry opponent, often aimed at sensitive anatomical locations..

D

Deuce Court. The part of the court into which you must serve whenever the score of a game is even; the term "deuce" is derived from an Italian phrase which can best be translated to mean roughly as much fun as playing tennis against Mussolini. The deuce court is still preferable to serving into the other court, which is called the ad court after the Latin phrase "ad nauseam," meaning roughly as much fun as playing doubles against Nero and Caligula.

Dink. The result of your effort to hit an overhead smash.

Dinkins, David. Former tennis-playing mayor of New York City who drove less athletic mayors of New York like Abe Beame, Ed Koch, and Peter Stuyvesant crazy by never missing a dink shot.

Double Fault. A definite gaffe or lapse in protocol committed at the interview for admission to the country club. The double fault derives its name from a notorious incident at the Merion Lawn Tennis Club when a candidate for admission tried to sell a used Pierce Arrow roadster as a new Bentley to a Main Line matriarch while noisily chewing away on several wads of Doublemint chewing gum. The salesman was blackballed from the Club, but ran off with one of the waitresses and several pieces of flatware. He subsequently gained his revenge on the tennis world by siring Ilie Nastase.

Duck. What you should try to remember to do when playing the net.

Duck Soup. What you look like when you fail to remember.

E

Eastern Grip. An affliction which causes great embarrassment on the tennis court. It is acquired by eating Oysters in months without an R in them and must be distinguished from the Western Grip, which results from drinking the water during doubles matches in Tijuana.

Egmont Overture. The piece of music it appears you are aspiring to conduct when you begin your service motion.

Exercise (verb). To move about on the tennis court, in a vain attempt to keep up with other players.

Exorcise (verb). To invoke the aid of the Roman Catholic Church to remove other players from the court.

Ex Post Facto. The polite Latin way of describing what has happened when you have run into one of the posts that holds the net up after the point is over; one of the hazards of the occasional attempt to run after a tennis ball.

F

Fault. A mistake when serving.

Fault-Finding. A typical conversation among tennis players, centering on characteristics of other tennis players who are not present.

Fault zone. Any portion of the court on which you happen to be standing.

Fifteen. For some reason, fifteen, rather than one, is the name given to the first point won in tennis game. Calling this point "fifteen" rather than "one" allows a player to feel that he or she has accomplished something more significant than standing flat-footed and calling his opponent's shot out. Many players feel entitled to deduct these extra fourteen digits from their age as the years go by.

Flotsam and Jetsam. What your tennis racquet and gear become when you hurl them into the lake and take up sailing.

Forehand. An emergency maneuver with a tennis racquet used to try to protect oneself from being hit by a tennis ball.

Forehand Volley. Shooting at the tennis ball when use of the racquet seems too complicated.

Forehead. That part of the player's anatomy struck by the ball when neither the forehand nor the forehand volley proves successful.

Fore. What to yell when your forehand sails so long that it reaches the golf course.

Fore and Aft. What to yell when your forehand sails so long that it reaches an ocean.

Forty Love. The number of mistresses or secret lovers one can recall if one (a) is a very lucky person and (b) has a very good memory.

G

Game. What someone generally says after winning four consecutive points from you.

Good get. Common all-purpose expression used to praise other players' level of hustle, determination, and ability to run after and hit the ball.

Good God. Common all-purpose expression used to describe your level of hustle, determination, and ability to run after and hit the ball.

Good shot. An upper, when you are tired. A downer, when you have taken too many uppers.

Grandstand. The seldom-accomplished feat of staying awake and upright while playing or even watching an entire tennis match.

Ground strokes. The manner in which one hits a tennis ball after it bounces, derived from the manner in which one stirs coffee. Consider the ball a latte if it is on the forehand side, an espresso if it is on the backhand side, and a regular with two sugars to go if it is above shoulder height; the manner in which the racquet is wielded should vary accordingly between that used to hold a demitasse spoon at a dinner party, a wooden coffee stirrer at office meetings, and a doughnut at a truck stop.

Gut. Almost as prominent as a part of one's racquet as it is of one's anatomy.

H

Hard court. How any court feels when you trip over your feet while running back for a lob

Har-Tru. The website address for articles about Harry Truman. A welcome respite from tennis.

Head racquet. A piece of equipment useful for returning balls aimed at one's head.

Hell or high water. (a) Being given the choice between playing tennis or whitewater kayaking over Niagara Falls. (Hint: Go for the kayak.); (b) choosing court time between the drought and monsoon seasons.

Higgins, Henry. Insufferably pedantic, self-centered English perfectionist in the play *Pygmalion* and the musical *My Fair Lady* who missed his true calling as a tennis pro.

Home Court Advantage. Suing your doubles partner before he or she sues you.

Hot Shot. Shooting your tennis partner before he or she shoots you.

I

Iks. Primitive people whose culture long ago broke down into anomie and mayhem. The people who invented tennis.

Ilie Nastase. Talented tennis player and linguist who translated curses, epithets, and derogatory comments in twenty-three languages to and from Serbo-Croatian while playing tennis against players of all nationalities. Called "Nasty" even by the Ik.

Iliad, The. A book attributed to Homer but really written by Ilie Nastase that described carnage, slaughter, and treachery caused by a woman. The world's first recorded description of mixed doubles.

In. A term used to describe the balls that other players, but not you, hit during the tennis match and the crowds to which others, but not you, belong when not playing tennis.

"I think I can, I think I can, I think I can." Including it helped the Little Blue Engine That Could sell a lot of copies so maybe it will help me. Saying it also helped the Little Blue Engine get to the top of the mountain. So maybe wearing blue tennis clothes and saying it will help your tennis. But don't count on it.

"I've got it." The third most often heard lie on the tennis court, after "Nice try" and "Sorry."

J

Jack Kramer. The trademark for what was for many years the standard wooden racquet made by the Wilson Sporting Goods Company.

Ultimately it was more lucrative for Wilson to license the name "Kramer" for use as the name of a character in a television series.

Joke. The one printable, four-letter word that can be used to describe your tennis game.

Jimbo and Jimbo. Jimbo was a nickname for Jimmy Connors and the over-sized racquet that he used, designed by the Wilson Sporting Goods Company so that it could sell replacements to the Jack Kramer racquet. As tennis racquets became more sophisticated and more expensive, the term "jimbo" became confused with the term "jumbo" when referring to racquets because of the over-sized loans needed to be taken out to pay for them.

Junk. What Harold Solomon and Eddie Dibbs hit and Vitas Gerulaitis smoked.

Junk pile. Where most Jack Kramer, Jumbo, and other tennis racquets end up after being used a few times on the court.

K

Ken. Doubles partner of Barbie and an opponent you might be able to beat at tennis on a good day inasmuch as he cannot move, is five inches tall, and has no racquet.

Kick. (a) What the junk that Vitas Gerulaitis smoked possessed; (b) what your serve does not possess, no matter how much junk you smoke.

Tennis, Anyone?

King, Billy Jean. A great player who did wonders for women's tennis and women's sports in general. Formerly Billy Jean Moffitt, she assumed her present name upon usurping the throne from Bobby Riggs in a match during which Riggs lost the horse he was relying on to allow him to move about the court. Scholars say that Riggs is called Richard rather than Bobby in the Shakespearean play based on these events because Shakespeare's spelling and handwriting were even worse than Geoffrey Chaucer's.

Knit-picking. Finding fault with other players' tennis attire, an indispensable part of most players' approach to the game.

Knees. A crucial part of the anatomy incapable of bending on a tennis court.

Kobak, James B., Jr. (a) The greatest writer about tennis or anything else who ever lived; (b) the wittiest person who ever lived; (c) the person you should thank by recommending this book to or, even better buying it, for everyone you know.

L

Laver, Rod. Perhaps the best male tennis player of all time.

Lengley, Susanne Longhorne. Perhaps the best female tennis player of all time.

Livingston, Doctor. Perhaps the worst tennis player of all time. The only player ever to have gotten hopelessly lost and to disappear for decades while changing ends of the tennis court.

Lob. A high shot which, if executed successfully, causes one's opponent to run around aimlessly; become temporarily blinded by the sun; strain, sprain, or otherwise injure most of the muscles in the head, neck, shoulders and one arm; and use the remaining arm to draft a motion to expel the lobber from the country club.

Love. A score of zero in tennis, believed to be derived from the French word for egg, *l' oeuvre,* as in the phrases you can't make an omelette without breaking eggs, you've got egg on your face, and you really laid an egg on that one.

Lost. The feeling experienced when on the court in a fast-paced tennis game.

Lost in space. The feeling experienced when on the court in a slower-paced tennis game during which someone hits a lob.

M

Marquis de Sade. Inventor of tennis. Also invented other forms of pain and humiliation, such as squash, handball, racquetball, badminton, volley ball, ping pong, and sex.

Match Ready. Preparing to build a bonfire out of accumulated tennis racquets and other quickly abandoned and useless tennis paraphernalia.

"Mine." (a) Something you fervently hope your partner will say on almost every shot; (b) something you should say if you spy any loose change on the tennis court.

Misérables, Les. A classic tale written by Victor Hugo to have something to do during change overs in tennis matches. In the novel Henri LeConte is hunted mercilessly for years in the tunnels under Stade Roland Garros by Yannick Noah for having mistakenly taken a brioche out of Noah's tennis bag during Davis Cup practice.

Mixed doubles. A game in which men are paired with women, husbands with wives, debutantes with fiancés, etc., in an effort to curb population growth.

N

Net cord. The thing to remember to pull on a parachute.

Net play. (a) One of the things to remember not to engage in during a tennis game; (b) in your case, an activity almost as dangerous as parachuting.

Newcomb. A game much superior to tennis in that the balls are large and never bounce, no racquets are involved, and the other players are generally disinterested middle schoolers participating only because their gym teacher requires it.

Newcomb, John. A popular former Australian tennis star famous for his mustaches, which intimidated children during youthful games of Newcomb.

No man's land. A phrase used to describe wherever you are standing on a tennis court. Not to be confused with the phrase "never, never land," which describes the tennis court itself.

O

On Dasher and Dancer, on Donder and Blitzen. What to say to cheer other players on as they run after the ball when you can't remember their names.

Open. What to do to a new can of tennis balls before playing with them. Playing with the balls still in the can places strain on the arm and damages the racquet.

Open Era. The 1960s. A time when people put almost anything in a can and then smoked it.

Out. Correct answer to the question, "Where did you go?" as in the dialogue "Where did you go?" "Out." "What did you do?" "Nothing," which can be used to describe the result of your tennis endeavors.

Outright winner. A good shot hit by a Republican, to be distinguished from an **outright whiner**. **Outright whiner** is one term, among many others that will not be repeated in a politically correct, family-oriented book such as this, used by the Republican to describe a lefty, pinko, tree-hugging liberal mistakenly allowed onto the tennis court.

Oxymoron. A logically inconsistent phrase such as saying "Nice match" and "I enjoyed it" to an opponent who is as big and dumb as an ox and just beat you six-love, six-love.

P

Pace. Amount of speed applied to the ball.

Pace yourself. What you should remember to do at the bar.

Play. Work, when what you play is tennis.

Pickleball. A recent invention combing elements of badminton, tennis, ping pong and leftovers from the Stage Deli.

Playpen. You have either been accepted to an Ivy League college in Philadelphia because of your tennis ability or, more likely, sentenced by a federal judge to play your future matches in the Eastern State Penitentiary in Philadelphia because your tennis ability is deemed to make you a menace to society.

Jim Kobak

Point. The basic unit of scoring in tennis; deceptively so named to make you think there is a purpose to running around all day chasing a little ball while wearing over-priced short pants and sunglasses.

Prince Racquet. An Internet scam involving the Royals. Do not under any circumstances send the thousands of dollars asked for in the emails to the indicated address. Instead, send them to me.

Q

Quality match. An extra-long match that guarantees plenty of time for even the most impatient and frustrated tennis player to reduce his or her tennis racquet to ashes in any wind conditions.

Quisling. A treacherous player who serves when others are not ready and substitutes a squash ball for the tennis ball.

The quick and the dead. An objective description of your tennis partner and you.

R

Rabid tennis fan. A tennis aficionado who has been bitten by a dog and likes to chew the balls.

Racquet head. A French mobster. Be sure to let him win.

Red clay. The color of a tennis court constructed by a Fauvist painter, to be distinguished from a **Red Klee** court, or court repainted by Paul

Tennis, Anyone?

Klee with funny little figures drawn in it as if one had done a singularly poor job rolling the court.

Roland Garros. The site of the French Open tennis championship; a tennis complex built on a pit of red clay to keep French laundresses employed.

Roll it over, Beethoven. What Beethoven's tennis coach yelled at him to do at the end of each practice session. The coach yelled so loudly and so often that Beethoven became deaf and moved to Vienna where there were no tennis courts to roll.

Rushing the net. What to consider doing in the dead of night, with a pair of scissors.

S

Seeded player. A successful, highly regarded player who has been produced by artificial insemination. Not to be confused with the seedy players with whom you most frequently consort.

Service break. What happens when the maid drops the china. A good reason not to take the good china to the tennis court.

Set. A principal unit of scoring in tennis, derived from the Egyptian god Set, a symbol of evil.

Slam. Making six no trump in bridge, a much better use of four players than tennis. Not to be confused with the **Grand Slam**, the most satisfying accomplishment in tennis, achieved by destroying one's racquet forever by applying it with force against a net post, backboard, or opponent's head.

Slice. The art of imparting spin to a ball by approaching it with a short but choppy swing as if you are hungry, it is a brie, camembert, or Gouda, and your racquet is a cheese knife.

Strings. The seldom used things that you see crisscrossing your racquet. No matter how many times you pluck at them they will not make music unless you remove them from the racquet and put them in a violin or a guitar. Your racquet will then have a hole in the middle, but this should be scarcely noticeable for your level of play.

Stroke. The manner of striking the ball, as in the phrases, "different strokes for different folks" (two players hitting the ball simultaneously), "beware of sun stroke and heat stroke" (neither player hitting the ball because both are looking directly into the sun), and "he had a fatal stroke" (one player killed the other).

Sweet spot. You have your hopes up, but this is a tennis book, not a sex manual. Sex has no place in tennis. Everyone is always too tired, the sunburns hurt too much, and none of the participants is on speaking terms with any other participant.

Tennis, Anyone?

T

Tennis camps. A polite name for distant places where children and sometimes whole families are transported for weeks of brutal torture while their bank accounts are systematically depleted. Tennis camps are known by other names such as Alcatraz, Andersonville, Dannemora and, when run by Club Med, the Gulag Archipelago or Guantanamo Bay.

Tennis drills. Serious practice, derived from a combination of the Norwegian word "ten," meaning I have had tendinitis since I was ten years old, and the Sanskrit "drill," meaning as much fun as ten root canals.

Tennis racquet. The business of selling expensive tennis equipment, such as racquets spelled with a q rather than k so that they cost more.

Tennis whites. For too many years, the only color of clothing or people allowed on many tennis courts.

Thirtysomething. Players' best collective effort at remembering the score or their ages.

The Three Musketeers. Nickname for the three famous pre-World War II French tennis players who, during difficult Davis Cup matches, stabbed their opponents to death, giving the clay at Stade Roland Garros its characteristic red hue.

Time. What the umpire says to get the players to leave their chairs and resume play.

Time and a half. What the umpire says to you, knowing how long it will take you simply to get out of the chair.

Topspin. The spin one wants to impart to a well-struck tennis ball to keep it within the bounds of the court. In your case, best achieved by putting the ball in the washing machine.

Tournament. A series of tennis matches designed to determine the best players in a manner producing the greatest possible amount of tedium, discomfort, and embarrassment.

Tourniquet. One of the things you (a) should wear to avoid playing in any tournament you may foolishly have entered or (b) will desperately need should you enter and foolishly play in the tournament.

U

Umpire. Someone who gets to sit in a chair during a tennis match. Did the umpire not have to remember the score and argue with John McEnroe, it would be the best job in tennis.

Underspin. Spin applied to a ball to make it stop suddenly.

Uppercut. Punch to use on someone applying underspin, or indeed any spin, to the ball.

Upshot. The act of hitting the ball high and softly to the player directly across from you at the net. The upshot is sometimes confused with the denouement, which is a polite way of describing the tracheotomy to remove the ball lodged in your throat after the other player has gleefully returned your upshot.

U Thant. A former Secretary General of the United Nations. U Thant took this position to avoid the strains and diplomatic tension of running a neighborhood tennis club.

V

Vale of Tears. Your side of the tennis court.

Valley of the Shadow of Death. The particular area on your side of the court where you are standing.

Vijay Amritraj . India's most famous tennis player. **Amritraj** once played Canadian doubles in Australia against Edith Piaf, a French woman, and John Lennon, an Englishman, in a match arranged by U Thant. This match is alternately referred to as the French and Indian or Seven Years War, as it went on for a long time, no one remembers who won, and John Lennon left to marry Yoko Ono and break up the Beatles before it was over.

Voyage to the Center of the Earth. The act of bending down to pick up a loose tennis ball.

W

Walkover. A forfeit. A walkover occurs when a player muffs three consecutive overheads, hurls his or her tennis racquet at the nearest object, and walks over to the bar to down innumerable margaritas, daiquiris, or whiskey sours, depending on the season and country in which the walkover occurs. Not to be confused with the **walk out**, which is what one's dates, fiancées and wives do.

Watch out. What to remember to say before throwing the racquet during a walkover.

Way out. Frequently heard expression on the tennis court, used to describe variously where one's shots have landed, what one's service motion looks like, and one's general style of dress and behavior.

Wooden racquet. Quaint, ancient piece of equipment believed to have been used by Dutch tennis players to strike wooden balls while wearing wooden shoes. The balls are now used for croquet, the shoes have become Birkenstocks, and the racquets are used chiefly to hang on walls to distract termites from eating the house.

Wrong foot (verb, transitive): To put one's tennis shoes on the wrong feet.

X

X-Country Skiing. (a) An activity almost as frustrating as tennis in which one may risk life and limb and endure strenuous exercise in bitter cold, but at least never has to bend down to pick up a ball; (b) the subject of *The Wimp's Guide to Cross-Country Skiing*, a much better investment than any piece of tennis gear, especially for the author.

Xmas Tree. Chopped down pine tree in your living room, which you fervently hope will not have a tennis racquet under it on Christmas day.

X-ray Machine. Standard post-match tennis equipment.

Y

Y Axis. The baseline, when the tennis court is viewed as a graph. If your movements were plotted against that axis, they would form a bell curve reminiscent of your physique but with only a random and infrequent log of the cosine relationship to the movements of the ball.

Yeti. A Sasquatch, big foot, or abominable snowman. A handy description for many in-laws, bosses, and tennis instructors.

Yin and Yang. The sunny and shady parts of tennis court, respectively. Together, they form an area the size of China, through which you are expected to chase tennis balls.

Yours. The most indispensable word in the tennis lexicon, used even more often than the word "Out." Using this word allows you to bask in a shady spot, inspect your nails, and avoid making a fool of yourself while your partner scurries about after the ball. Most tennis novices fail to understand that the word "Yours" can scarcely be uttered loudly, quickly, or often enough. With enough practice, you should be able to shout it to players on other courts when you are playing singles.

Youth Movement. Read on. Both these words ceased to have any application to you many years ago.

Z

Zen. State of enlightenment best achieved in tennis by standing motionless at the net and being hit repeatedly by tennis balls while simultaneously developing sunstroke.

Zero sum game. The result of most of your matches.

Zip. What your serve should have on it, but won't.

Zipped up. What your tennis shorts should be, but aren't.

Zippy. What the repartee after the tennis match should be, but isn't.

About The Author

James B. Kobak, Jr is also the author of the Wimp's Guide to Cross-Country Skiing and the novel Up Front from Behind as well as a forthcoming children's book, Eric the Skier. He is a contributor to the HumorOutcasts website whose essays and articles have appeared in many publications.

www.ingramcontent.com/pod-product-compliance
Lightning Source LLC
Chambersburg PA
CBHW020934090426
42736CB00010B/1137